G.R. Williamson

Willis Newton

Willis Newton

Books by Author

Texas Pistoleers: The True Story of Ben Thompson & King Fisher

Frontier Gambling: The Games, The Gamblers &   the Great Gambling Halls of the Old West

G.R. Williamson

Willis Newton

The Last Texas Outlaw

G.R. Williamson

Indian Head Publishing

Willis Newton

First published 2013

ISBN-13: 9780985278021

ISBN-10: 0985278021

LCCN 2013906087

Front and Back Cover Design

In Association with

INDIAN HEAD

PUBLISHING

Dedicated To:

Jean Ann Williamson

(The toughest woman to ever thread this planet.)

Contents

Introduction

It was a damp, chilly morning in March of 1979 that I knocked on Willis Newton's door in North Uvalde. A slight drizzle was falling on me while I waited for a response. I knocked again and called out his name. After a minute I heard a raspy growl, "It's open. Come on in."

Stepping inside the rundown clapboard house with the unkempt yard, I saw a small withered looking old man glaring at me from his rocking chair. "What the hell do you want?"

"Mr. Newton, I am the guy that called you yesterday and wanted to ask you some questions."

"I ain't talking to no one about my life. I'm going to sell that to Hollywood for a bunch of money."

I knew then that doing an interview with the old outlaw was going to be a tough nut to crack. As best I could, I reminded him of our phone conversation on the previous day when I asked him to provide me with some details on how to rob a bank or a train. I told him I was writing a paperback novel (which was true) and that I needed some help in portraying a factual description of how the robberies took place (which was also true). After a few moments of consideration he gestured to a chair in the small living room and agreed to answer "just a few questions."

In contrast to the chilly weather outside, it was hot and stuffy in his cluttered living room—being heated by a small gas wall heater. I quickly unloaded my tape recorder and after a brief conversation with Willis, handed him the microphone. I asked him how to stage a bank hold up and what was involved in robbing a train. Then like turning on a wind-up toy, Willis essentially started telling me his life's story. From time to time I managed to get in additional questions but for the most part he rattled off the well-practiced accounts of his life in machine gun fashion—rationalizing everything he had done, blaming others for his imprisonments, and repeatedly claiming that he had only stolen from "other thieves."

I had no idea what to expect when I stepped into his little house that day but what I encountered was the quintessence of the criminal mind. Everything he had done was justified by outside forces, "Nobody ever give me nothing. All I ever got was hell!" As I listened in rapt attention he sat center stage speaking in a high-pitched raspy voice, pontificating on an assortment of subjects of his choosing. Lacing his speech with large quantities of profanities, vulgarities and racial slurs, Willis was quite articulate in telling his stories – a master of fractured grammar. At times he would slip into mythological story telling mode where he would talk of killing rabbits and camping out while on the run from lawmen. Then with a little prodding he would return to the basic facts of his story.

In the process, he told me how he was raised as a child and how he was first arrested for a crime "that they knowed I didn't do." He went into detail about his first bank holdup, how he "greased" a safe with nitroglycerine, robbed trains, and evaded the lawmen that came after him. Willis described the Texas bank robberies in Boerne, San Marcos, New Braunfels, and Hondo (two in one night). He also related the double bank robbery in Spencer, Indiana and proceeded to give accounts of bank robberies in a multitude of other states.

Eventually he recounted the events of the Toronto Bank Clearing House robbery in 1923 and finally the great train robbery outside of Rondout, Illinois, where he and his brothers got away with $3,000,000 in cash, jewelry, and bonds. He went into great detail about the beatings he and his brothers took from the Chicago police when they were later captured. As he told the story his face reddened and his voice rose to a pitched screech until he had to pause to catch his breath. Then lowering his voice he described how he managed to negotiate a crafty deal with a postal inspector for reduced prison sentences for himself and his brothers by revealing where the loot was hidden.

He told about his prison years at Leavenworth and his illegal businesses he ran in Tulsa, Oklahoma, after he got out of prison in 1929. He complained bitterly about being sent back to prison in McAlester, Oklahoma, for a bank robbery "they knowed I didn't do," in Medford.

After returning to Uvalde, Texas, following his release from prison,

Willis swore that he "never had no trouble with the law after that." When I asked him about his elderly brother's botched bank robbery in Rowena, Texas, in 1968, he exploded, "They tried to get me as the getaway driver but hell, I was in Laredo, over 400 miles away! I had 12 witnesses that said I was there the night old Doc and R.C. got caught."

At the end of the interview I asked him to comment on the Rondout loot buried in Texas by his brother, Jess. He said he knew where it was buried—just not exactly where because "Jess was whiskeydrunk when he hid it." Looking at the frail aged man dressed in a frayed union suit and a pair of stained pants, Willis did not appear to have any loot left from any of his robberies; although, locally it was rumored that from time to time he would spend money that appeared to have been printed during the '20s or '30s.

Finally, I turned off the tape recorder and thanked him for helping me with the details I needed for my paperback Western. Returning to my car, my mind was awhirl with the stories I had just heard. The thought of writing a book on the old outlaw had never crossed my mind and I was very sincere in telling him I was a fiction writer and not a biographer. But what a story he told!

The following week I put the cassette tapes in a safety deposit box thinking the information might be useful for a future writing project. A few years later I transcribed the tapes, added my notes and filed the interview away. Then while working on another book I came across the interview file and knew I had to write his story—but the complete story, not just what Willis had told me in the interview. As I found out this was a much bigger project than I had anticipated. I tracked down several hundred newspaper and magazine articles on Willis and his brothers, court records and police reports. Then, where I could, I interviewed the few remaining people who actually knew and had firsthand knowledge of Willis Newton.

Along the way I unearthed some startling evidence that dispelled the myth that Willis and his brothers had never killed anyone in the commission of their numerous crimes. This is the first time that this fact has been brought to light.

When I had finished the research I knew I could write his story. With some minor editing, culling some of the blatant racial references and over abundances of profanities, I tried to keep his words to me intact. I do not espouse demeaning racial terms regarding any ethnicity of people—whether it is the Irish, Jewish, Hispanic, African, Italian, or other deprecated populaces.

In a few instances I had to restructure his accounts for clarity. He spoke in a rapid fire jailhouse prose using a wide range of criminal jargon that sometimes was difficult to follow. Wherever possible I strove to retain his colorful phraseology, using the common expressions of the day.

In writing Willis' story, I omitted most of his repeated self-justification for his actions in which he took great pains to paint himself as a gallant criminal—in the Robin Hood vein. It is true that he robbed from the rich but he gave very little to the poor. In a few of his accounts, he did describe giving the "hard money" (silver coin) to some poor and downtrodden farmer that had helped him. In addition, he repeated the idea that he never meant to harm anyone in the robberies; "all we wanted was the money." There is no doubt that Willis Newton was shaped and stamped by the rough economic conditions of the southwest in the late 1890s and early twentieth century. Yet at the same time, there were hundreds of thousands of other people that strived to work hard and become solid citizens of their communities. It was his choice to go after the "easy money."

In poring over hundreds of newspaper reports and magazine articles I was struck with how much of the story varied with what Willis had told me, sometimes substantially. At the same time I found that the newspapers, in their rush to get their story out, misspelled names, got their facts wrong, under or over estimated dollar amounts of loot taken, and had a very difficult time keeping the Newton brothers' names straight—Willis and Wylie (aka Willie or Doc) dealt them fits. Quotes from the actual newspapers used in this book reflect exactly what the public read with all the errors, inverted and confusing sentence structuring, and copious use of commas intact.

Then, as I was writing the book, I interviewed R.C. Talley. At 92, he still had a clear recollection of his involvement with Willis Newton and he provided a detailed account of the events of the bungled bank robbery in Rowena, Texas in 1968. Though Willis was in his mid-70s at the time, Mr. Talley described him as the mastermind of the heist.

Then, when things went sour, he told how Willis left him and Doc Newton alone to face a violent shoot-out with the Ballinger police.

So what follows is not a glorification of his criminal career but rather, the true story of the last Texas outlaw—Willis Newton.

Willis Newton—early in his criminal career, decked out in new clothes and boots.

The Early Years

The First Bank Hold-Up

"Why if you don't get caught, then you're innocent!"

Willis Newton rode a horse to his first bank hold up in Boswell, Oklahoma. The year was 1916 and he was 27 years old. By this time "Skinny" Newton was well on his way to becoming one of the most successful outlaws in American history. He had already been arrested for numerous crimes, served prison time, and robbed a train.

In 1916, vast portions of rural Texas and Oklahoma were still very similar to wild days of the Old West. Sam Bass had been shot up and killed in a bank robbery in Round Rock, Texas, 38 years earlier. Jesse James had only been buried for 34 years. Thomas E. Ketchum (Black Jack Ketchum) had been hanged in 1901 for attempted train robbery. Robert LeRoy Parker (Butch Cassidy) and Harry Longabaugh (Sundance Kid) were reported to have been killed by the Bolivian police in 1908. Frank James had died the year before (1915), spending his last days giving 25-cent tours of the James' farm in Missouri. The Dalton brothers were all gone except Emmett Dalton, who had survived 23 gunshot wounds in the ill-fated double bank robbery in Coffeyville, Kansas, in 1892. He served 14 years in a Kansas prison and then moved to California where he became a real estate agent, raconteur, author, and Western actor. He died in 1937 at age 66.

At the time of the bank robbery, Willis did not know that over the course of his life he would rob more banks and trains than all of his predecessors combined. He and his brothers still hold the record for the most money stolen in train robberies in U.S. history. According to Willis he was "just trying to learn the ropes" in the Boswell holdup.

It was in Durant, Oklahoma that Willis met up with a loose-knit band of bank robbers. One of them asked him if he wanted in on a daylight bank job. "Hell yeah," Willis told them and he was introduced to two men he would work with in the Boswell robbery.

"One was a tall, slim boy named Charlie Rankins and the other guy—I don't recall his name but he had a face full of scars, probably smallpox or something. They had horses and we planned up the Boswell bank job; it was about 15 or 20 miles this side of Hugo.

"The bank was the last building in town as you were leaving, Nothing but brush after that. They had some trees there that you could tie up horses. Well, that's what we done; one day we went over to Boswell and tied up the horses at the bank. Nobody knowed me there so I went on in and acted like I was getting change. Charlie and the other feller come on in as I was talking to the cashier. I threw down on him and hollered for everybody to 'stand pat because we was robbing the bank.'

"While I kept the front, Charlie and the other guy run around behind and started sacking the money. Charlie got all the money out of the safe and the other guy cleaned out the cash drawers. It come to $10,000. We told everybody to stay put or we would blow their damn heads off. Then big as you please we untied our horses and slowly trotted off into the brush. Nobody come out of the bank when we looked back.

"We headed across the South Boggy River and we followed the river to just outside of Hugo where we split up the money. I give them my horse and saddle and said, 'You fellows go on and I'm going into Hugo tonight and catch me a train out of here.' I figured they wasn't looking for no one to be catching a train, they was looking for three men on horseback. I knew there was a passenger train that left there sometime after 10 o'clock, so I stayed out there in the brush 'til it got dark.

"They took all the hard money (silver) and give me green money (cash) for mine, so I put it around my waist and folded some in my pocket. When I put my coat on you

couldn't tell I had it in my pockets or anything. Just before 10 o'clock come I walked in there and bought me a ticket to Ardmore, slick as you please. It was clear sailing after I got to Ardmore."

About a month after the Boswell robbery, Charlie Ranking was arrested when they found a quantity of silver dollars in paper rolls bearing the bank's name. When Willis learned that his friend was in jail he devised a plan to get inside the jail and see if he needed help. He knew a man in Hugo who had been a stool pigeon in prison. Visiting with the man, he boasted that there seemed to be a number of easy banks in the area that "needed to be knocked over."

The man immediately went to the police and reported his conversation with Willis.

"When I went down to the depot that night to catch a train, the law was laying for me. They grabbed me and put me in jail, which was just what I wanted. So then I got to talk to Charlie and I said, 'You want me to help you? I can come in and turn you out if you want me to.'

"No, hell,' he said. 'I don't think they've got much on me, not enough to put me in the penitentiary. They'll be setting my bond in three weeks.'

"They kept me jailed for three or four days and just wouldn't turn me loose. They could keep you in jail just as long as they wanted to, in them days. Finally, I had to go get a lawyer and paid them $250 to get out of jail. Later on, I found out they sent Charlie to the penitentiary at McAlester for 25 years. I never did see him again.

"My cut from the robbery was right around $4,000, but I didn't have it on me when I came back to Hugo. I had come down to San Antonio and put six or seven hundred in the bank and I give them lawyers a check on the San Antonio bank to get me out. Well, about two months after that I went down to San Antonio to draw the rest of my

13

money out and they had the law waiting for me. I had wrote a check to get my money and this teller says, 'Well, wait here a minute.' He took it and went back there and I seen him talking to somebody and I knowed they were going to arrest me. So I just walked off and went down to Uvalde and give a little lawyer a check for all of my money, and he went up there the next day and got it. I never did know what they wanted to arrest me for, but that's what they was fixing to do. They arrested you for nothing in them days. They would do anything they wanted to you.

"The bank in Boswell was the very first daylight job I ever done for money. But I didn't hesitate. Hell, if you hesitate you're liable to get in trouble. You go to do anything like that, you better do it. I always told them, 'Let's go boys,' and I took the lead and we never stopped for nothing. The bank robbery at Winters, Texas, with Frank, the old bank robber, was my first night job. We never got but $3,500 in Liberty bonds from there, though, and they killed that one old boy there alongside the car. So I never got nothing out of that. He had the bonds in his hip pocket, the one who got killed."

Boswell bank building as it stands today.

Willis' version of his first bank hold up has a reference to a botched night time robbery in Winters, Texas, where he and three others broke into the bank at midnight. Frank, a friend of his, had been told that the Winters bank had a vault that they could blow with nitroglycerine. His source was a Banker's Association detective named Boyd, who wanted a cut of the loot. As it turned out after they had blown the vault door, the money was stored in a round safe that they could not open. After ransacking the vault they finally left with $3,500 in Liberty bonds.

Heading back to Abilene, a third man named Al was driving an early model Hudson when the car got stuck in sand and burned out the clutch near Buffalo Gap, Texas. They abandoned the car and hid out in the hills until the next night when they walked into Buffalo Gap. Just as they neared the town, a car full of lawmen passed by them on the road. When the car stopped and turned around Willis and his friend, Slim Edgarton, ran for the brush while Frank and Al stood their ground shooting at the lawmen in the car. After a volley of shots Al took a slug in the chest and went down. Frank then took off in a different direction into the brush. It was the man named Al that had been carrying the bonds when he was shot and killed by the posse.

Willis managed to escape but was later caught with his friend Red, near Sweetwater. They were jailed in Ballinger with Slim Edgarton, who had been caught earlier. After bribing the sheriff's wife, the trio managed to break out of the jail in the middle of the night and get away.

Repeating a pattern he would use throughout his career, Willis returned to San Antonio after the Boswell job and then headed for the family place in Uvalde. In 1916 he was still "learning the ropes" of the outlaw life while, with exception of his brothers Jess and "Doc", the rest of the family was engaged in honest labor—working as ranch hands or hard scrabble sharecroppers, known in West Texas as "cyclone farmers."

Son of a Cyclone Farmer

"We never stayed in one place for more than a year, even if my daddy made a good cotton crop. He was a cyclone farmer, always looking for a honey pond and a fritter tree."

Willis Newton was born on January 19, 1889, near Cottonwood in Callahan County, Texas. He was the sixth child of 11children that Jim and Janetta Pecos Anderson Newton raised as dirt-poor sharecroppers. They moved from one location to another, hoping to find the perfect spot to eke out a living, usually growing cotton. The West Texas term for their life style was "cyclone farmers" because "they blew all over the country, looking for something better."

When any of the Newton children were old enough to tote a cotton sack down the "middles" they picked cotton—for their parents or other farmers. Ivy, Bud, Henry, Dolly, Jess, Willis, Wylie ("Doc"), Bill, Tull, Ila, and Joe all picked cotton, chopped firewood, or shot rabbits and squirrels to keep the family going. As teenagers, the boys had to learn how to hook up a mule to a plow and work the cotton rows. At the same time, the sisters had to help with the cooking and "boil their clothes" in a large kettle outside their shack. They hung them out to dry on a line that was strung out to the windmill.

Willis' sister Ivy died with measles when she was a teenager giving birth to a child and his brother Henry died when he was 16 of "inflammatory rheumatism that affected his heart". They died in 1899, four months apart.

Jim Newton, his dad, had an insatiable wanderlust. He was never satisfied with their location—moving the family around Arkansas and Texas, always in search of the perfect place to raise cotton and his kids. Willis said that they never stayed more than one year in any place until 1903. He was always saying, "Well boys, we're going to turn over a new leaf and off we would go." Sometimes not more than a few miles down the country.

Because of the hard life they endured and the constant moving,

Willis had a low opinion of his father, saying, "They said my daddy was a good man but sure as hell nobody could ever say what he was good for! He drug us all over the country."

Whenever Jim Newton had some money he would buy some land and start farming, usually cotton. "The old man bought 160 acres of land on Turkey Creek for about $1,000. He really paid $100 or $200 down but he could never get it paid for; he'd run out of money and then let it go back. He always owed everybody so we never had nothing."

Willis told of his dad's callousness toward the family's plight, particularly his mom:

> *"When I was twelve, me and Doc helped my mother work a small piece of land raising cotton while my daddy was working at a gin over in Cottonwood. We plowed the cotton and kept the weeds out. At night we would have to chase the cows out to keep them from eating the cotton plants. We got a bale that was worth about fifty dollars and my mother was going to use it to buy our clothes and stuff for Christmas.*

> *"We took it over to the gin and just left it in the cotton yard. When we got ready to sell it in Cisco we'd take a wagon over there and they'd load it for us. We was going to have plenty of money to buy things that year.*

> *"But no! The old man came back from Cottonwood and went to Cisco first. He stopped by the cotton yard, loaded up Ma's bale of cotton, took it to Cisco, and sold it. I had been picking cotton for some other folks and I had to go to Cisco with him.*

> *"There was nothing I could do. Pa used that cotton money to pay a debt he owed. He stole Ma's money and that was that.*

> *"I remember my mother broke down crying when I told*

her what Pa had done. 'We worked so hard for that bale of cotton to get our winter clothes and something for Christmas—and then he took it.'

"Most years Ma only got 10 or 12 dollars to buy us kids all of our winter clothes. She'd buy the cloth to make our clothes and she made them with her fingers – with a needle and thread. She didn't have no sewing machine until after I left home."

Later that year, Willis stayed behind when his father and Jess went up to New Mexico to cut timber in the mountains near Cloudcroft. With his overbearing father gone he decided he wanted to go to school.

"I'd wanted to go to school but the old man always had something for us to do. So, soon as he had left, I told my Ma I was going to the school that was about two miles down the road from us.

"My mother made all of my clothes—a little old shirt and a pair of pants. I didn't have no shoes but I did have a worn-out coat that a lady give me. It was in the winter but here I went. I never had nothing to take with me to eat so I would take a sack with me that may have had some meat and bread at times. I'd always go out in the brush at lunch so the other kids wouldn't know I didn't have nothing.

"In a week or two I could read everything in the first reader. I didn't have no spelling book but the teacher, Miss Dora Norton, bought a second hand speller and give it to me. Pretty soon I was running off and leaving them other kids—reading and spelling.

Then Miss Dora said, 'Willis, get your mother to get you a second reader.' When I told her we didn't have no money to buy books she bought me a second reader herself.

"Miss Dora taught me arithmetic, and soon I could divide, multiply, add, and subtract better than the rest of the kids. Then she gave me a third reader and finally a fourth grade speller, a little before I had to quit school."

Finally when Willis' clothes were so thread bare that he was ashamed to go to school he quit school, three weeks short of a complete semester. When the teacher met his mother on the street in town she asked why he had quit school after being such a good student. His mother explained that he did not have any decent clothes to wear and was ashamed to be seen by the other students. The teacher's response was, "He's the smartest pupil I ever had in school in my life. If you give him an education, there's no telling what he'll do. And if you don't give him an education, there's no telling what he will do."

Willis could always count on his mother to stand up for him and felt that she tried her best to raise her brood of children. When possible she would read stories to her kids—outlaw stories. She once told him, "Willis, I guess if I had been a man, I'd a-been a bank robber or outlaw too." She read every outlaw story she could find and then re-read them over again when she had nothing new.

Listening in rapt attention, Willis fondly recalled his mother's stories:

"She had a pretty good education; I think she went to the seventh or eighth grade in school.

"I'm the only one of the kids that took after my mother. She read every outlaw story that come along—Jesse James, Billy the Kid, the Daltons, the Youngers. She didn't read nothing but outlaw stories until my sister and brother died. After that she read the Bible. She would read three or four stories and then she would tell us kids about them at bedtime."

After he had mastered reading, Willis thrived on newspaper accounts of criminals of the day. Reporters at that time wrote the exploits of Harry Tracy with heroic flourish leading many poor Americans, as well as the impressible boy from West Texas, to believe Harry Tracy was a modern day Robin Hood.

"The first outlaw I can remember alive was Harry Tracy. In 1902 him and David Merrill escaped out of the penitentiary in Oregon. Went over the walls. Every Saturday I'd read the Chicago Blade and the Saturday Ledger. There'd be a story about Harry Tracy and I'd read it.

One of the stories told how Tracy and Merrill had a falling out and shot it out in a duel. They agree to walk 10 steps and then shoot. Tracy turned at nine and killed Merrill.

"The law chased him all over Oregon and Washington. I seen several times where they had him cornered and he'd grab somebody, throw him on his back, and then get away. They wouldn't shoot and he'd just get away. He was a big, stout fellow and he kept on the run until someone on a farm snitched on him.

The law surrounded him in a barn. They hollered for him to come out and by damn he did! He jumped out of a window; broke his leg and then he crawled off into a wheat field. They was scared of going in there after him so they just waited.

He wasn't going to get caught by the law so he just killed hisself."

Harry Tracy—Willis Newton's outlaw hero.

Contrary to Willis' blind admiration for Harry Tracy, the truth is Tracy was nothing more than a two-bit thug that was glorified by the press to sell newspapers and magazine. His real name was Harry Severns and was said to have run with Butch Cassidy and the Hole in the Wall Gang.

On March 1, 1898, Tracy and three accomplices engaged in a gunfight at Brown's Park, Colorado. They killed a member of the posse named Valentine S. Hoy. Later Tracy and an accomplice of the Brown's Creek gunfight were captured. They escaped in June 1898 from the Aspen Colorado Jail but late in 1901, Tracy was captured, convicted, and sent to the Oregon State Penitentiary.

Tracy and a convict named David Merrill escaped on June 9, 1902, shooting and killing prison guards and three civilians in the process. The size and scope of the manhunt and the extensive media coverage of the day solidified his claim to infamy. He dodged the law and evaded capture for a month, hiding out in the remote area near Seattle, Washington.

On June 28, 1902 he killed his partner Merrill whose body was not found until July 14. Then on July 3, 1902, he set up an ambush near Bothell, Washington, where he killed a detective, Charles Raymond, and a deputy John Williams during a shootout. This prompted The

Seattle Daily Times, July 3, 1902, to patently proclaim that:

> *In all the criminal lore of the country there is no record equal to that of Harry Tracy for cold-blooded nerve, desperation and thirst for crime. Jesse James, compared with Tracy, is a Sunday school teacher.*

Fleeing, Tracy took several hostages in a residence and shot it out with lawmen. During that shootout he killed posse members Cornelius Rowley and Enoch Breece.

Tracy's luck ran out on August 6, 1902, in Creston, Washington. He was cornered and shot in the leg during an ambush by a posse from Lincoln County, resulting in his being badly wounded.

By the time Sheriff Gardner arrived Tracy had crawled into a nearby wheat field. Finding himself surrounded, Tracy shot himself in the head to avoid capture. During his 58-day crime spree, Tracy killed seven men. At the time of his death, he was 28 years old.

Of all of the press coverage afforded Harry Tracy, Willis took great pride in his hero's reported challenge, quoting him as saying, "I'm Tracy. I don't want to hurt anybody but those who get in my way, and when I say put your hands up, put them up."

In many ways that is how Willis modeled his life. He was often quoted as saying, "I never wanted to hurt nobody. All I ever wanted was the money."

Jim Newton—Willis Newton's father.

Janetta Pecos Anderson Newton—Willis Newton's beloved mother.

The Brothers

"I wanted something, and I knew I would never get it following a mule's ass and dragging cotton sacks down them middles."

The Newton family moved to Crystal City in January of 1906. After wandering around West Texas and Oklahoma for the previous 20 years Jim and Janetta loaded everything they owned into a wagon and a small buggy and headed south. Jim and the women rode in the wagons while Willis and his brothers walked.

"We moved down to Uvalde on the last day of December in 1906. We stayed all night in Albert's Wagon Yard. The next day we was at a Cross-S auction in Uvalde and were asking around about work. They told us how to get to Crystal City. They said to go to the Jackson ranch, three miles this side of Crystal City."

The rancher was drilling a water well on his property and he hired Jim Newton and all the boys. They camped out and worked on the digging project for about a week. When they could not produce a working well, the man paid them off and the family returned to Callahan County. After a year the family returned to Crystal City, which at the time was little more than a series of tents with only two permanent buildings.

The Cross-S auction that Willis spoke about was the lure that enticed Jim Newton to pull up roots and head for his next Utopia. Two land speculators, E. J. Buckingham and Carl Groos, had purchased the La Pryor ranch and all 96,101 acres of the Cross S Ranch in 1905—which at the time was one of the largest ranches in the United States. By 1907, the ranch had been surveyed into sections and each section divided into 10-acre farms. Purchasers of a farm gained title to a town lot in Crystal City.

Jim Newton had undoubtedly read the Cross-S hand bill (reproduced below :)

Cross-S-Ranch

FERTITLE LAND MORE VALUBLE THAN GOLD

The great Flood Tide of Immigration is Swiftly Drifting to Southwest Texas and the eyes of the thirsty investor are now on the Cross-s Ranch, in Dimmitt and Zavala Counties, Texas on the head waters of the artesian belt, where the flowers bloom from spring to spring, and where the expense of the farmer is reduced to the minimum and the results of his labor is the best that nature will produce.

We will place you on your home lot in the town of Crystal City and your farm in the fertile valley of the Nueces River free from malaria, insects and Negros, for $10.00 cash and $10.00 per month, without interest.

Located 40 miles south of Uvalde and 50 miles from the Mexican border, Crystal City was promoted as a perfect farming area with fertile soil, mild climate, and an abundance of pure water (Nueces River and easily-dug artesian wells.)

As with other over-hyped developments in this part of Texas, Jim Newton found that though it held promise it certainly was not the *land of honey ponds and fritter trees.*

> *"Before we moved back, Doc and I hopped a freight train and made up a camp on the Nueces River outside of Crystal. I had a Winchester and Doc had a pistol. He shot another boy accidentally but it didn't amount to much. A guy came out to our camp and said, 'You boys have some telephone calls wanting you in town.' We went into Crystal but before we did I told Doc to go over to old man Thompson's place and leave the pistol there.*

"When we got to town the sheriff came over to arrest me for carrying a pistol—hell, I was carrying a Winchester not a damn pistol. It didn't make no difference, they got my rifle and was taking us to jail when I said I had to go to the toilet. I knowed the fellow that went with me and I talked him into making out like I took off running and he started yelling while I was still in the john. Doc took off in the other direction but they finally caught him and took him to jail in Batesville.

"On the way over to Batesville that night Doc jumped out of the car and walked back to Crystal. The law caught him just outside of town. Meanwhile I went back and got the pistol from the Thompson place."

Willis hid out for over a month and then talked with a friend who had seen Doc in jail. The friend said the locks on the jail were easy to saw through with a hacksaw. Willis immediately went to Batesville and freed his brother. After that they hid out in a tent near the Thompson house until they were both captured again by the sheriff. While in jail Willis claimed, "Doc and I both come down with typhoid fever, like to killed us!"

In contrast to Willis' account, the *Zavala County Sentinel* newspaper gave a slightly different account of the pistol-carrying arrest. In a small article in the September 9, 1909, edition read:

Notice of Newton brothers release from jail.
The Zavala County jail is again unoccupied, the two Newton boys having served out the amount of their fines of $100 each for carrying pistols. They left here Saturday afternoon for parts unknown. They came here from Eastland County.

How much of Willis' account is self-aggrandizing embellishment is open to speculation but one thing for sure is that it was during his early days in Crystal City that Willis and his brother Doc started to tire of honest work in favor of "easy money." In a *San Antonio Evening News* article dated November 14, 1924, Willis was described as *a youth that made considerable reputation for himself as one of the meanest boys in the community, stole an old sow and her litter of baby pigs. He evaded arrest and punishment. "I got away with that," he said to himself. "Why can't I keep on doing it? Why work when stealing is more profitable?"*

Doc Newton

Wylie (Doc) Newton

Doc (whose real name was Wylie but often reported as Willie) was big, strong, and a fearless man with little common sense. Willis blamed a bite from a rabid wolf for Doc's behavior.

> *"It was when we first got to Crystal City and we was digging water wells. We was camped out one night and he woke up screaming, 'A mad wolf bit me.' It was either a coyote or wolf had stood on his chest and took a bite*

out of his head. My parents sent him off to Austin for one of them 'hydrophobic treatments' and after that he just wasn't right. For the rest of his life Doc had no more judgment than a little kid. Whenever he really got hot, he would commence to slobbering and say, 'My damn head hurts.' He couldn't help it; the damn wolf did it to him."

It was this peculiar behavior of Doc and a rush to judgment by the law that Willis blamed for sending him to prison the first time.

"Every son of a bitch knowed I was innocent. They knowed I didn't break no law!

"My daddy had a cotton crop down outside Crystal City and after he done picket it all out and he came back to Crystal City. He had 700 pounds of cotton left in the field, piled up.

"He told Doc to get a wagon, haul it off, and sell it and give it to a man he owed 20 dollars."

Doc did as he was instructed and after noticing the wagon was only half full, pulled into the next field and filled up his wagon. The following day Doc drove the wagon down to the gin and sold the wagon load to the operator. Willis claimed that he was not with Doc when he sold the cotton.

The first he saw of Doc that day was when he met him for breakfast at the hotel in Crystal City. While they were eating they saw two cotton men looking over Doc's borrowed wagon.

Willis told his brother to go hide out in the privy behind the hotel while he went outside to see what the men wanted. They immediately arrested him for the stolen cotton and they later captured Doc and placed him in the same cell. Continuing Willis' account:

"Now about three nights before that they had burglarized a post office at Cross Plains. They had a boot track and a shoe track as evidence. Now me and Doc had

boots just alike and when they were having my examining trial the sheriff from Callahan County come over there and measured my boot and says, 'that's it.' He hauled me over to jail but the next day they caught the other guy that robbed the post office and he told them it was Doc who done it with him—not me, so they had to turn me loose.

"Doc was in jail but I managed to get a hacksaw up there to saw one of the window bars. That night Doc and the other boy got away. So there was three of us running from the law.

"Now they were tracking us with blood hounds and later that night, we caught us a horse and cut across a field and come up on a fence. The law was waiting for us. They took us back to Rusk (prison)."

There is no way to describe the Texas State Prison at Rusk other than "a hell-hole." At that time it was basically a slave labor prison where the convicts faced endless days of harsh and sometimes lethal working conditions. The prison made pig iron and finished implements for commercial sale.

The original blast furnace was the 25-ton, charcoal-burning "Old Alcalde," given the nickname of Governor Oran M. Roberts, who had pushed for the penitentiary. Later, a second furnace, the more efficient 50-ton, coke-burning "Sam Lanham," replaced the Old Alcalde. Water-pipe foundries and a cast-iron foundry completed the Rusk iron works.

In addition, the prison used convict labor to raise cotton and vegetables to bring in revenue and feed the prisoners. A few years before the Newton brothers had arrived, the prison labor force had finished building a 25-mile railroad line between Rusk and Palestine, Texas. Its purpose was to bring in raw materials for a prison iron foundry and to take the finished products out.

Convict work detail at Rusk Prison.

The convicts were housed in a two-story sandstone and brick cell house that had 528 double-bunked cells that could hold 1,056 prisoners. A brick wall, 20 feet high and 30 inches deep, enclosed the seven-acre site.

Willis made several references to "the Walls" when he talked about his years of incarceration at Rusk.

> *"Them guards were mean sons of bitches! They had them old 'bats' with steel handles on them that had a thick, six inch leather strap on the end—six feet long!*

> *"They'd just lay you down and beat the shit out of you! They'd stomp your head and beat the guts out of you!*

> *"Yeah, they was mean alright; just plumb mean!"*

Ball and chain leg shackles used at Rusk Prison. At the top is one of the
brutal "bats" that guards used to beat prisoners into submission.

Both Willis and Doc were convicted and sentenced to four years in
the penitentiary. There, Doc knocked a guard off his horse and let
more than 100 prisoners, including himself, escape. Other breakout
attempts pushed Doc's sentence to 10 years.

*"Then they transferred me down to the Sugar Land farm
unit where I done 30 months. Finally I was able to get a
letter to my ma to come see me. I told her to go to the
governor's office. 'You just go in there and sit down like
you are waiting for someone. There will be a man
standing by the door to the office. You wait until he
moves away a little and then you run in quick.'*

*"She got in and when they tried to pull her out, Governor
Colquitt said he would talk to her.*

*"Ma told him all about my case and when he said he
would turn me out pretty soon she said, 'No, I'm going to
stay right here in this office. I've got a cotton crop to pick
and I need him to pick cotton. I'm a widow woman and I
ain't got no one else* [which was a lie.] *I'm going to stay
right here.'*

"The governor saw what he had on his hands and gave in

*to my ma. He told her to go home and that he would have
me out on a pardon in two weeks. And he done it.*

*"Governor O.B. Colquitt was the man that finally
brought a halt to those damned beatings and civilized the
Texas Penitentiary.*

*"That's when I got out. I got that pardon and went to
West Texas and went back to picking cotton."*

--------•••••••••••••--------•

Jess Newton

Jess was the wild one—always looking for a good time. Charming
and irresponsible, he was two years older than Willis. In spite of his
many drinking sprees, Jess had earned a reputation as a master
horseman, and at one point traveled with Booger Red's Wild West
show.

In June of 1903 after returning home from Stephenville, Willis asked his mother the whereabouts of his brother Jess.

> *"Ma said, 'They got him in jail over at Eastland.' Jess had been working for a man that ran fighting roosters. When he got ready to come home he picked out a couple of them game roosters and brought them with him. The law caught him with the roosters, threw him in jail, fined him 20 dollars, and made him work it off fixing roads and city streets at 50 cents a day.*

> *"He run off once but they come and got him at our house. They put him back to working on the streets—and the funny thing is they was paying a man three dollars a day to watch him work and not run off. Now where's the sense in that? Anyways in a few days Jess come walking in."*

It was in 1907 that Jess started working for Booger Red's Wild West Show. He had a number of minor brushes with the law; mostly related to drinking and fighting, but did not join Willis and Doc in looking for the "easy money." He was perfectly satisfied to break horses and raise hell in the drinking holes.

He even served a brief hitch in the 350 Infantry of the U.S. Army during World War I. He was discharged as a private.

Joe Newton

Joe Newton was born on January 8, 1901, in Cottonwood, near Abilene. He was the last of Janetta Newton's brood and was a good-hearted, friendly charmer who really just wanted to be a cowboy. When he was 6, the family moved to the mesquite flats and prickly pear territory south of Uvalde.

"We came here in covered wagons from North Texas on the first day of January in 1907. I was just about to be 6, the baby. There was Jess, Willis, Doc, Tull, and me. Tull was a cowboy all his life. It was the rest of us that got into trouble."

While Willis was involved in a series of petty crimes and eventually into armed robbery, Joe was working hard to be a top of the line cowboy. He spent most of his time around ranches and figured he would for the rest of his life.

"One or two of my older brothers was cowboys, and that's all I ever wanted to be, just a cowboy, so I turned out to be a pretty good one."

That all changed in 1920 when a flood wiped out a ranch in West Texas where he was working as a ranch hand. ``About that time, I got a letter with two $20 bills in it from my brother Willis. He told me to come to Tulsa because he had a good job for me.''

Joe put his saddle and rigging in burlap bag and caught a train to Tulsa. Willis was there to meet him. Later, Joe told the story this way:

``What`s that?'' demanded Willis.

``My saddle,'' said Joe.

``What the hell you doing with a saddle?''

``You said you had a good job for me. The only thing I know is cowboying.''

``Throw that damn thing away. We`re going to rob some banks.''

``That don`t sit well with me, Willis.'' "They shoot people for robbing banks.''

``We ain`t going to get shot.''

Willis gave Joe a handful of $100 bills and said, "Stealing from banks wouldn`t be like taking money that actually belonged to somebody. It would all be insured. Hell, everybody knows that them banks and insurance companies are nothing but thieves. Nobody would get hurt.''

"Them $100 bills did more than anything to sway me over. I went out and bought me a suit or two and, although I`m a Baptist, I decided to go with him. Willis was always popping off about me being `a damn good Baptist.'''

Willis Newton (left) and his little brother Joe in expensive suits.

The Banks

"I robbed over 80 banks. I robbed about 20 banks before my brothers came along and we robbed 60 banks."

By late 1919, Willis felt like he had "learned the ropes" and was ready to form his own gang. He had come to the conclusion that most of the men he had worked with were dim-wits, idiots, bumblers, or down-right cowards. It was while he was working under a man named, Frank, that he finally had had enough.

> *"We was over in Michigan just before Christmas in 1919. Frank was inside the bank when he heard a noise and just turned around and shot his own man. Hell!*
>
> *"Well, we had to drag him to the car and the car was about 150 yards away. We got into the car, and he said, 'Boys, I can't go. I don't know whether I'll live. The best I can get is five or ten years and I don't want to get you fellows in trouble. Just leave me behind.'*
>
> *"So we left him and he hollered for help, but he died right there for no damn reason!*
>
> *"Well then on the very next bank in Texas the bastard almost shot me! Hell, I had enough of Frank so I struck out on my own—with people I could trust."*

Though he did not prefer the term, "gang" he brought in the only people he could truly trust.

> *"Well, we wasn't no gang. We was just brothers working together in a business. I was the one that got us all together and I was the one that knowed all the angles. I was the head man of that business, and I give the orders,*

38

so I never did mind being called 'old man.' And when I give my brothers orders, they turned out to be real reliable. They done it and didn't go helty-skelty."

Occasionally, Willis had to recruit other men for specific bank jobs, notably Herbert S. Holliday and Brent Glasscock. Holliday was a seasoned criminal who usually worked as the "outside man" (lookout) or get-away driver.

Glasscock, on the other hand, was an "inside man" who specialized in blowing off the doors of vaults or safes with nitroglycerine—in the trade a "grease man." Working with the explosive liquid evidently made Glasscock a very nervous man who was prone to frequent ulcer attacks.

Though Willis and his brothers did periodically pull off a daytime robbery, their preferred method was to break into a bank in the middle of the night and blow the safe. Glasscock eventually taught Willis the art of using nitroglycerine to "peel a safe."

"Stop up all the cracks with cup soap—all the way around. Then on top make you a little cup out of soap where you can pour your grease (nitro) in. Then you would put your cap and string in and set it afire. In those days you could find grease plentiful up in Oklahoma where they was shooting all them oil wells.

"We'd get a gallon can of it and then go out and bury it. Then when we needed some we would go out and pour us up a pint. The way you do it is to put a shot in and blow off the first plate then more shots to get through the other plates—usually steel, then rubber, then steel again.

"Nitro only shoots one way—out. So you don't burn no money inside. Dynamite blows everyways."

Willis Newton became an expert safe cracker when he learned how to use nitroglycerine to blow the doors off square or rectangle safes.

Willis bribed a corrupt official with the Texas Association of Bankers to supply him with a list of banks that used an older model of safes that could usually be blown with nitroglycerine. At that time most banks in the big cities had gone to safes with round doors that were so tight that nitro could not be forced into them—which rendered them untouchable to the Newtons. Small towns, especially those in Texas and the mid-western states, had not updated their safes and still used the old-style square or rectangular safes.

Using the list as a roadmap, the Newton lined up a string of banks and went into business. Their usual tactic was to operate in small towns and in the dead of winter. They would usually cut the telephone lines and try to locate the night watchman or constable before entering a bank to rob it. Two of the brothers would usually stand guard with shotguns to hold off anyone aroused by the bank blasts.

*"I robbed over 80 banks. I robbed about 20 banks before
my brothers came along and together we robbed 60
banks. We robbed 30 or 40 banks in Texas. We robbed
plenty of banks in other states like Illinois, Arkansas,
Missouri, Kansas, Wisconsin, North and South Dakota
and several other states. In 1922, we took a swing out
west and took a few banks around Portland. Then we
come across to Butte, Montana, and sold the get-away
car and took a train back to Tulsa."*

Actually, the gang robbed banks in Texas, Arkansas, Oklahoma,
Kansas, Nebraska, Iowa, Colorado, North Dakota, Missouri, Illinois,
Wisconsin and Canada. They were suspected of having robbed banks
in Washington and Oregon, but it has never been proven.

The Newtons always used the latest models of Studebaker or
Cadillac as their get-away cars. For speed and dependability the
brothers thought the Studebaker Big Six touring car could not be beat.
The vertical six cylinder engine could provide speeds of up to 80 miles
an hour—faster than most of the Model-T's used by lawmen of the
day. In addition, the four-door sedan was designed with plenty of
room, up to seven passengers. Joe Newton was a master at using the 3-
speed transmission to evade the law and make their escape after a bank
job.

Whether it was a daylight stickup or a night time break-in, the
Newtons always went armed with handguns (mostly Smith & Wesson)
and shotguns (usually Remington .12 gauge pump or automatic.) Willis
was very emphatic about the gang's use of firearms.

*"We used what we could get but we liked Smith &
Wesson double action .44 revolvers—didn't like them
automatics because they jammed a bunch. We liked
Winchesters and .12 gauge Remington automatic
shotguns. We kept the shot guns with birdshot in the
barrel and buckshot in the magazine. The first shot was
meant to scare the shit out of them and the next load up
would have killed them. So we made it a point to have
birdshot in the barrel and buck in the load.*

"We didn't want to hurt anybody. We planned everything to make sure we would not have to shoot anyone unless it was to save our hides.

"We were just going for the money. We figured we didn't want to hurt nobody. Our aim was to get in and get out. We didn't want no shootouts with police or nobody else.

"When you kill a man, that's all there is—it's over. But when you steal from him, why he can go out and make more money."

In keeping with Willis' assertion that he and his brothers were strictly "businessmen—like lawyers, doctors, or bankers", he portrayed banks and insurance companies as being no different than them in that "it was just one thief stealing from another thief." Although they took all of the cash they could find in a bank, it was the unregistered "bearer bonds" that provided the bulk of their loot from the heists.

"We would have starved to death robbing banks for the money; it was them Liberty or Victory bonds. They was "bearer bonds"—paid to whoever cashed them, just like money. We could get 90 cents on the dollar for them. I had five places in Chicago where them bankers would buy every bond I brought to them. They all knowed that they was stolen but they didn't care. Tell me what is the difference between them and us? They was crooks just like us."

It was the habit of the Newtons to eventually take a train back to San Antonio, where they lived the high life until they had spent most of their loot. *"We stayed in the Menger Hotel in San Antonio, we always went first class living in nice hotels, driving nice cars and dressed in high-dollar suits. In Chicago I stayed at the Blackstone hotel, their best rooms."*

G.R. Williamson

Arma, Kansas

In May of 1919, before Willis formed his own gang, he worked the last job with "Slim" Herbert Holliday. They hit a bank in the small coal mining town of Arma, Kansas, which was located 120 miles south of Kansas City. Willis said that Herb's brother Frank accompanied them to the home of some "Dagos" that lived just outside of Arma. Other than the racial slur applied to Italian and Greek immigrants he did not supply any names of the men he worked with in the burglary. In his account he used the term "rank" which refers to lawmen or the law.

> "Slim said he knowed some Dagos that lived in Arma so him, Frank and me went over there and planned up us a Sunday night job. Slim was a nervous sort, kinda jumpy. He told Frank to stay on one side of the street and me on the other to work as lookouts. He said, 'You boys seeing anyone walking around with lights you better figure they've spotted us robbing the bank. They'll go around and wake up everybody.'

> "Slim and the Dago went into the bank with a pick to knock into the concrete vault. It was a little old four inch thick vault. First Slim stepped up and gave it a few licks. He couldn't dent it so he hollered for Frank to give a try. Frank whacked at it for a minute and then he gave up on it too. The Dago asked for a shot at it and then before you know it he had a hole caved in it. The two of them climbed through and come out with a stack of Liberty bonds.

> "About the time that they had the bonds stuffed into a handbag, Slim got spooked. 'We got rank (law officers)! They're going from house to house waking people up.'"

Willis knew immediately that it was not lawmen but rather the next shift of miners going to work with their helmet lights on. They were smoking and quietly talking—with no alarm.

43

"But old Frank said this was his operation and he said, 'We got all the money we will ever need here and we're leaving.' Wasn't much I could do so we took off.

"Come to find out, the newspapers said that they didn't know the bank had been robbed until eight o'clock the next morning. When we counted up we had $65,000 in Liberty and Victory bonds. But the hell of it was we had left $200,000 or more in the vault. We would have been all rich, right there, but no, that damn coward Frank left $200,000 just sitting there in the bank.

"We come back to Tulsa and cut up the money and bonds. Frank said he knew where we could get a good deal on the bonds in Memphis so him and me went over there but all we could get was $.75 on the dollar and we had over $10,000 apiece. I always got $.90 on the dollar or I would walk away."

This episode galled Willis at the thought of leaving $200,000 in cash behind at the bank. His rancor continued a few weeks later when Frank shot a new gang member that spooked him during a night robbery. A short time later, he was finally convinced that he was working with incompetents and cowards when Frank almost shot him after a Texas robbery.

Deciding it was time to start his own outfit he wrote a letter to his brother, Joe, to join him in Tulsa and then contacted Jess and Doc to come a running because they were going to make a bundle of "easy money."

Omaha, Nebraska

Before Jess and Doc arrived in Tulsa, Willis contacted Brent Glasscock, the "grease man," to join with Joe and him to pull off some jobs just outside of Omaha.

"There was just three of us then. That's when I took charge. I told Joe to stand guard outside with a shotgun and then I told John (Glasscock), 'Now I'm going inside with you, and I want you to show me how to shoot it.' He told me how to do it and stood there watching. So I fell to it and shot the drum door. It blowed and we got all of the money and come on out."

While Willis and Glasscock were inside the bank, Joe stood outside in the darkened street. Before the blast he saw a farmer approaching in a wagon and he raced up to stop the man before he reached the bank. Pointing his shotgun at the farmer he said, "Now, mister, I want you to hurry up and get out of the way. We're going to rob this bank here tonight."

The man did not believe Joe and he started to slap the traces to his team. Just then, Willis touched off his very first load of nitroglycerine and not only did it blow open the vault door but blew out the front window of the bank. The explosion shot shards of glass into the street in front of the farmer's wagon. Shocked, he turned his team down a side street and took off in a dead run.

Joe jogged over to the bank found Willis and Glasscock stuffing a handbag with cash and bonds. Willis said they had it all and was headed out of the bank when Joe saw several bags of silver coins. "We ain't leaving them, are we?" The get-away car was over a half of a mile away and Willis said that they would leave the hard money. It was Joe's first robbery and he hoisted one of the heavy sacks over his shoulder. About half way to the car Joe stopped to catch his breath. "Drop the silver," Willis told him. "Come on, we've got to get out of here." Joe would not give up the heavy bag of coins and struggled on to the waiting car. Even though the bag contained close to a thousand dollars in change that was the last time Joe wanted to shoulder silver coin away from a robbery.

A few days later they hit a bank in Glenwood, Iowa, and found that most of the vault contained Liberty or Victory bonds ($300,000 to $400,000) that were worthless because all of them had been registered. Infuriated, Willis piled the bonds in a stack and burned them in the vault.

It was Joe's silver coins that led to their arrest later after a hotel maid spotted them and some pistols in their bags. The police had pegged them for holding up a movie theater in Des Moines, Iowa. After bribing some of the lawmen with money and diamond stickpins Willis got the charges dropped and they were free men again.

While they were in Des Moines, Willis met his future wife, Louise Brown, who was working at a department store. At the time he was using the alias, H. S. Scott, and Joe was using the name of Rogers. According to Willis' account, the woman was engaged to marry the man who had identified Willis as the movie theater bandit. The night of the robbery she had been playing cards with Willis. Convinced that the man was trying to frame Willis, she told the man to go to hell and turned her full attention on "Mr. Scott."

Hondo, Texas

After Doc and Jess joined the gang they set their sights on robbing a bank in Hondo, Texas. On January 9, 1921, the gang drove into the small town 30 miles west of San Antonio to rob one of the two banks in town. It was just past midnight and the temperature was near freezing.

The Newtons knew the night watchman in Hondo, and as was his habit, they found him huddled around a pot-bellied stove in the depot. They cut all of the telephone wires and then went back to check on the night watchman. He had not budged from his spot by the stove so Joe was placed across the street as a lookout while the rest went to the bank.

> *"Sometime you just get lucky 'cause they had left the vault door open. They had left it unlocked so we didn't need no nitro or nothing. We jimmied the window, walked over to the vault, tried the handle and she opened! You would be surprised how many times them banks would just close the door so it looked locked during the night.*

*"We had the vault cleaned out in no time and went to see
if the night watchman was still in the depot. Sure enough,
he was reading a magazine and drinking coffee by the
stove. Well hell, we figured we had plenty of time so we'd
go over to the other bank and give it a try. I kept Joe and
Doc watching the night marshal while Jess and I went
down to the other bank.*

*"We got inside that bank and cleaned it out. Damn, two
banks in one night and the night marshal, he never come
out of the depot!"*

The local newspaper, the *Hondo Anvil Herald,* carried the story with
a splash headline:

Yeggs Rob Hondo Banks
One of the Most Daring Robberies Ever
Staged in Texas Occurred Here
Sunday Morning

The people of Hondo were amazed and angered
Sunday morning when it became known that
both banks had been entered by yeggs, between
midnight and daylight, and robbed of both
money and valuables. Entrance to the First
National Bank was effected by forcing the
front doors; while the entrance to the state
Bank was effected by prizing down the bars
over the last window in the alley between
Parker's and the bank.

[Copy of the actual newspaper headline.]

The newspaper went on to give an elaborate description of the robbery:

> Owing to most of the money in both banks being in the money safes, with time locks set, the loss in cash was not serious, the First National losing a total of $2,814 while in the matter of actual cash loss the State Bank was a little more fortunate, its loss being $1,879; both banks losing a total of $4,694 nearly all of which was silver coin.
>
> The funds of both banks were covered by burglary insurance, consequently neither will suffer loss. *[Just like Willis had assured his brothers.]*
>
> Owners of private boxes, who had put their valuables in the vaults of the banks, are the heaviest losers, and their actual loss will not be definitely known for some time—probably a month—as the owners of the boxes are the only ones who can clear up the loss, the officials of the banks not being advised of the contents of the boxes.

The safety deposit box owners had cash, government bonds, War Savings Stamps, jewelry, and other valuables in their boxes so it was impossible to determine the exact amount taken in the robbery. Estimates of as high as $30,000 were never confirmed.

The article continued to describe the "safe experts:"

> ...That the robbers were experts is borne out by the fact that they were able to work the combination on the vault of the First National Bank. *[Willis said it was left unlocked.]* They were also experts in the use of explosive, the vault doors of the State Bank being blown open by one of the most powerful explosives known— TNT *[Remember Willis never used dynamite— only nitroglycerine.]*
>
> The vaults were thoroughly ransacked and the floors were strewn with papers about two feet thick.

From the thoroughness with which the robbers made their search for securities it is evident that they spent two hours or more in the vaults of the banks and the private boxes of the customers are in a sad plight, most of them showing that they were beat open by some heavy instrument, probably with a sledgehammer that had been stolen from the blacksmith shop of Mask & Co.

...That the robbers were no tyros (archaic word meaning beginners) in the business of robbing is again borne out by the fact that they took every precaution against being apprehended by the possession of jewelry, gold coins, and so forth, which might lead to their identity. The floors of the vaults were literally strewn with such articles as might lead to their detection. Notes and other articles of value that could not be turned into money were cast aside and left behind.

It is generally believed that the band was composed of from six to eight men, and that both banks were robbed simultaneously, a gang being assigned to each bank.

Another circumstance that indicates that the robbers were not new to the game of bank robbing is borne out by the fact that every telephone line in town was cut, apparently, before the banks were robbed. And this part of their plans was carried out most effectively and by an expert telephone man.

...Cables were severed, apparently with saws, and single wires were cut with wire clippers. Only three telephones connected with the local exchange were working Sunday morning.

The robbery was discovered by the night watchman about five o'clock Sunday morning and immediately reported to Deputy Sheriff C.J. Bless.

...Harry Crouch, our local telegraph operator, was summonsed and messages were sent east and west in an effort to intercept the robbers, but as far as the general public is advised, nothing was learned as to the direction in which the robbers went.

Interior of the First State Bank of Hondo, Texas.

First National Bank of Hondo, Texas as it stands today.

Detectives from San Antonio and the surrounding area converged on the Hondo banks searching for clues to the duel-heist robbery.

> ...One of the most remarkable coincidences of this whole business is that these robberies could have occurred right in the heart of the town and not more than 200 feet apart, and not one among our people being any the wiser until daylight it was revealed what had transpired, and that too, it was since developed that the night watchman and the two other men were in the waiting room of the depot, not more than sixty yards from the front doors of the First National Bank, while the robbery was being accomplished. The robbers must have done their work very silently to avoid detection. *[It is hard to image a "silent" explosion of nitroglycerine.]*

The word the newspaper used for the night burglars was "yeggs," a popular vernacular expression of the era. It is interesting to compare the newspaper reporting to Willis' account in which the vault of the First National Bank had been left unlocked and they used nitroglycerine (rather than TNT) to blow the vault door on the State Bank. Even more interesting was the fact that there were no follow up articles on the robbery. There was not a single mention of the multi-bank burglary over the ensuing months—although it contained large advertisements from both banks. It was as if both banks had never been robbed.

The *Galveston Daily News* on January 10 reported the robbery describing a "clew" that proved to be a red herring:

Robber Heel May Lead to Arrest
Telephone Connections Cut When Banks at Hondo Are Looted

> San Antonio, Texas—January 10—A rubber heel, lost from a shoe, may lead to the identification of the bank robbers who made a successful haul of $20,000 from the First National Bank of Hondo and the Hondo State Bank early Sunday morning.

> The bank robbers gained entrance to the two banks by prying the iron bars loose from rear windows of the buildings and manipulating the

combinations of the vault in the First National Bank, but blew off the door of the vault in the state bank.

The haul was made from the safety deposit boxes in both banks, the robbers obtaining only $1,500 in cash from the First National and $29,350 of the state bank's money. The smaller vault safes in both institutions were untouched.

The balance of the loot, it is estimated by officers at the two banks, was secured from owners of safety deposit boxes in the banks. Hondo was not aware of the visit of the bank robbers until almost noon Sunday, when the open windows at the rear of the two bank buildings were discovered.

Heel lost in bank.

Sheriff J.S. Baden, during his investigation was given the lost rubber heel, which had been found in front of the vault of the First National Bank. Further investigation disclosed a set of burglar tools consisting of a pipe wrench, saw, and chisel, which had been left by the robbers. These however are not considered as important for they are of a standard make, easily purchased at any hardware store.

Just outside of the window through which the robbers entered the state bank, Sheriff Baden found the numerals 13,555 scratched on the brick work. This, bank officials believe, indicates the amount the robbers secured from the deposit boxes in the bank. *[This curious piece of information appears to have been just another "red herring."]*

Sheriff Baden believes the robberies were committed by a band of six men, who sent an advance guard of two into Hondo last week.

...Hondo citizens, who were up at an early hour Sunday morning, reported to the Sheriff that they saw a high-powered automobile leaving the outskirts of town occupied by six men. These, the Sheriff believes, were the Hondo robbers.

[Ironically] Sheriff Baden suffered a loss by the

early morning visit of the robbers, as his safety deposit box in the First National Bank was broken open and $300 in stamps and $150 in bonds were taken. A $100 Liberty bond, the property of his son O.J. Baden, of Donna, was left in the box.

In light of the erroneous "clews' the Newtons were never tried for the Hondo bank robberies.

Boerne, Texas

Shortly after the Hondo heist, the Newtons hit the Citizens State Bank in Boerne, Texas on February 8, 1921. Boerne was a small German farming community about 30 miles north of San Antonio.

"We had been living high on the hog at the Menger Hotel and then we decided to slip up to Boerne and rob the Citizens State Bank. It was a little bank but we come "away with over $12,000 in bonds and cash.

We caught a cold norther blowing in and we didn't have any trouble. We caught the night watchman when he was walking up the street. We tied up his hands and Joe stayed with him, keeping him in the dark so's nobody would see him. I shimmied up the telephone poles and cut all the lines and then we went down to the bank.

"We didn't even have to blow the safe there. The wind was a-blowing so loud nobody could have heard it anyway. After we finished up at Boerne, we took the night watchman with us and headed toward San Antonio.

"We took him out in the hills up there and give him a blanket. I told him to build a fire because it was going to be a hell of freeze that night. He was good old boy and he didn't give us no trouble. I told him to stay there until

daylight and then he could come out on the road and get a ride."

On February 9 the *San Antonio Evening News* covered the story:

Boerne Bank Is Robbed of Bonds
Night Watchman Is Forced to Witness Operations of Bandits

San Antonio, Texas. February 8—Forcing the town night watchman to accommodate them at the point of pistols, and after cutting all telephone wires leading out of the place, four heavily armed robbers today tunneled [tunneled?] their way into the vault of the State Bank of Boerne and stole $10,000 worth of liberty bonds and $500 in small change.

Following the robbery and with Paul Menn, the captured town watchman as their prisoner, the quartet fled toward San Antonio. The robbers are now hiding in this city.

Nine miles from San Antonio on the Foch Highway, which leads to Boerne, the robbers kicked the captive watchman from the automobile in which they were making their escape.

Mr. Menn was brought to San Antonio by local officers in order to identify the robbers if they were caught here.

The robbery of the bank was not discovered until seven o'clock this morning when Mrs. Mary Watts, in charge of the exchange at Boerne, found all telephone wires leading out of the place to have been cut.

Investigation of the robbery this morning by authorities at Boerne and by a squad of police under Chief of Police Munncy, who rushed to Boerne from San Antonio as soon as the robbery was reported, showed that the looting of the bank was undoubtedly done by the same gang which on January 10 last, broke into and looted the First National and the State Bank of Hondo of $20,000.

Because the robbers were foiled in their attempt to open a big safe in the bank vault into which they had tunnel more than $125,000 that was in the steel receptacle was saved.

Then on February 14 the same newspaper reported:

Sleuths Strike Snag in Search for Bandits
Hope of Connecting Two Men at Dallas with Robbery Fails.

...Man hunters charged in the search for the quartet of bandits who early last Tuesday morning tunneled their way into the Boerne State Bank, and stole $7,000 in Liberty Bonds and cash, today were reported to be at a complete standstill in their current investigations.

With approximately a week elapsed since the robbery, officers in the case this morning declared themselves to be practically without clues and without any additional suspects either under arrest or under suspicion. Evidence of connecting up the men taken late last week as suspects in the Baker Street post office robbery, and Boerne and Hondo bank robbing cases said to have fallen flat after a half dozen employees in the robbed Dallas post office failed to identify them as members of the Shriver Luna Rowan gang.

Investigations here of the activities of the two suspects is said to allow that they had no connection with either the Boerne are the Hondo jobs.

...All authorities in the hunt for the robbers have practically given up hope of any of the bandit quartet being identified by either Paul Menn, Boerne night watchman, who was kidnapped by them, or the Negro, Norman, who claimed to have talked to two of the robbers a few minutes before they looted the bank. *[Willis never mentioned the black man.]*

Boerne State Bank building serving as an antique store many years later.

A month later, the Newtons were at it again in Pearsall but got foiled by some long winded Texas Rangers.

> *"We went down to Pearsall to rob a bank one night; I believe it was in March of 1921. There was two banks there, but in one of them, the safe sat on the floor and we couldn't blow it.*
>
> *"A passenger train come in there about midnight and while it was there making noise, I climbed up the telephone pole to cut the wire. The pole was beside the telephone office right across from the bank. I cut them wires with a hack saw. Then when I run down the post, a pistol fell out of my coat and hit the sidewalk. Damned if it didn't land on the hammer and went off. It's a wonder it didn't hit me somewhere. But with that train there making noise, nobody heard anything.*

"The safe stood out in the middle of the floor. It was one of them big old Packer safes I had figured it would take maybe two shots of nitro and we'd be in.

"Two guys was talking at the depot and when they come up to the town, we seen that they was Texas Rangers. They had got off there; don't know what for. It was about one o'clock in the morning and they couldn't find a hotel open so they sat down on one of them high curbs across the street from the bank. They rolled cigarettes and talked. We figured they'd move on after a while but there they sat, just talking."

Willis and his crew sat watching the two Texas Rangers blowing smoke rings and generally chewing the fat until 3 in the morning. Then, figuring sometimes it's best to just walk away, they silently slipped away from Pearsall and returned to San Antonio.

Canadian Banks

In 1922 Willis and his wife Louise took a trip to Kansas City where they were staying at a first-class hotel. A friend of his from Chicago and his wife met them in the hotel. Then the two couples spent the summer driving through a section of Canada, scouting banks.

"So here we go up to Canada. We located a town named Melita, another named Moosomin and a third named Ceylon and figured we could blow the safes in each town. All three towns were about 100 miles from where we was staying near Pelican Lake in Manitoba.

"In late September 1922 we went up to Melita, cut all wires and grabbed the night hack and took him with us up to town.

"The bank was one of them big old two-story buildings and in those days nearly every bank in Canada had someone who slept upstairs over the vault at the back of the building. I blew that first shot and knocked the door out of there and a man upstairs started hollered, 'Let us out of here! Let us out of here!'

"I told the man, 'You stay up there in your bed and you ain't going to get hurt.'

"The bank was a Canadian Bank of Commerce, and you had to go through a bunch of plates to get in. It took me five shots to peel all of them off the door. When I put in the last shot I run out the door and the man heard me so he comes down the stairs. When the shot went off he screamed and ran back up stairs.

"About that time somebody showed up outside and one of our guys hollered to him to go back. When he didn't, they cut loose with some birdshot close to him and he got the hell out of there.

"After we blowed the safe we got all the money and headed out on the highway with our lights off. A little ways out we let the night hack out and took off in the dark.

"We got a few bonds and about $10,000 in cash. About a week later we went to Moosomin. We couldn't find no night watchman so I went in started on the vault. It was one of them big steel safes so I give her an extra shot— about 4 ounces and blowed the first door off. It come off clean and then I had to get the inside door to come open. It's called the "keister" and it took me five shots to get it open.

"There was one package of money. A little silver money was in some sacks in there and there was one package of

$6,000 American. That's all we took, we left the Canadian (currency.)

"When we come out there was a fellow shooting at us with a rifle. Joe angled around and put a round of birdshot at his feet. He took off like a scalded cat. Then all hell broke loose when some train man started tooting his damn whistle. The job had taken a whole hour and we was lucky we come out alive."

A month later, Willis and his gang hit their third bank in Canada.

"We hit the third town, Ceylon, and didn't have no trouble there. After that we left Pelican Lake and went down to Toronto. We found us a real easy bank; I took the door off with a single shot. But I almost got killed doing it. The guy we was working with ran off with the light just after I lit the string on the safe. It was pitch black and I couldn't see how to get out of there. I knowed I had about 15 seconds before she would blow so I jumped up on top of the safe and held the grease bottle close to my chest. I figured I was a goner when she blew but the blast only stung my feet a little. See, nitroglycerine only blows one way—out. Dynamite blows every which a way.

"We got about $10,000 American from that bank. Then all of us went back to Chicago where we lived high on the hog until we come back to San Antonio in the winter of 1922."

Gallatin, Missouri

The Newtons were back at robbing banks in 1922, this time in Missouri. Gallatin was a small town fifty miles north of Kansas City and it had two banks. The new bank had a round safe so that left the First Nation Bank, with a square Steel Pete, as the target. In addition to the brothers, Willis used a man called "Des Moines Billy."

"It was sometime in November and we had marked the bank in Gallatin Missouri, a little town north of Kansas City. We went up there and figured out a getaway. Then in a few days, sometime after midnight, we went into the First National Bank. I took along an old bank robber named 'Des Moines Billy' so I put him over across the street behind another bank as a lookout.

"I put Joe and Doc outside to cover the rest of the street. I went in and blowed the vault door, clean through the window. It was about two o'clock and across the square you could see lights and people at a hotel.

"We had cut the telephone wires so nobody could call out but damned if those idiots up at the hotel didn't start shooting.

"I went to work on the little square Steel Pete and it took me three shots. About this time an old watchman came down there and Doc hollered at him, 'Get back in there!' Just as I ran out the door Doc cut down on him with bird shot. He whirled around and started back the other way. I fell in right behind him and jammed my pistol in his side. I took his gun and brought him back down to Doc.

"Joe was up the street a block and he only had a shotgun so he couldn't do much about the people shooting from the hotel across the square. Doc also had a pistol and was shooting back at them.

"I went back in the bank and sacked up the money and when I come out of the bank I signaled for old Billy over there in alley. He didn't signal back so we went over to check on him and there he lays, shot to shit. A slug hit

him in the side of his head and killed him stone dead.

"Two of us drug him down the alley and out to the car we had waiting. We took off and in a little bit we stopped and put him in the brush because we were going to have to take a ferry to get across the river.

"We took the ferry and went to Kansas City where I knowed an undertaker. I give him $500 and he took a coffin down to where we had hidden Billy. He buried Billy the next day but I don't know where.

"After that we come on down to San Antonio for the rest the winter. We stayed at the St. Anthony Hotel most of the time."

Strangely enough 53 years earlier, just past noon on December 7, 1869, Frank and Jesse James rode into Gallatin and walked into the Daviess County Savings Association. Jesse went up to the counter and asked the cashier, John Sheets, to change a $100 banknote. As the cashier was writing out a receipt for the bank note, Jesse and his brother drew their pistols and each shot the cashier. Sheets sank to the floor with a large bullet hole in his head and chest.

The James brothers had thought Sheets was Union Army Major S. P. Cox, who had killed "Bloody Bill" Anderson. The brothers had ridden with Anderson, the brutal Confederate guerrilla, and swore that they would avenge his murder. After killing the cashier, they scooped up what money they could find and rode out of Gallatin.

At the edge of town Jesse's horse spooked and threw Jesse out of the saddle. Frank swung around and jerked his brother up behind him on his horse as the citizens of Gallatin opened up with a hail of gunfire. With bullets whizzing all around them, the pair rode off to become legendary outlaws of the American West.

Now, five decades later, the Newton Gang had ridden into town in a Packard automobile, robbed the First National Bank and fled amidst a roaring gunfight. The Missouri newspaper, *Moberly Monitor Index*, did not fail to cash in on the James boys connection and ran bold banner headlines.

Bandits Loot Gallatin Bank
Towns Citizens Held at Bay While Gang Blows
Vault and Gets $200,000 in Bonds and Notes.

ST. JOSEPH, Mo., Nov. 23.—The most thrilling bank robbery since the days of the James and Younger Boys in Missouri was that at Gallatin, Mo., early today, when six bandits robbed the First National Bank of $1,000 in gold and currency and overlooked $10,000 in cash in the vault.

Loot totaling several thousand dollars in cash and Liberty bonds, besides $200,000 in registered notes, was obtained by six bandits who, after blowing open the vaults of the First National Bank here, escaped before daylight today.

Scores of citizens, attracted by three blasts in the bank, were held at bay by two of the robbers, who swept the town square with a shotgun fire until the robbery was completed and the bandits escaped. Upon hearing the first explosion at the bank, Mayor Tate aroused five men and they approached the building. When they were within half a block, the bandits on guard opened fire on the five. Twenty shots were exchanged, while Tate stood behind a telegraph pole. Then the mayor's squad attempted to get to the bank through an alley, but was again fired on and a buckshot struck Tate.

The interior of the bank was completely wrecked by the explosions and many telephones in the town were put out of commission. Some of the wires had been cut by the robbers, who also cut the telegraph wires, delaying outside communication several hours. The robbers were on the job almost an hour. The people of Gallatin had not yet recovered from their amazement over the daring of the robbers, who held about 100 citizens at bay with a barrage of gunfire laid down during the blowing of the vault and the safe. It was one of the quickest jobs on record, and although so many of the townspeople had been aroused and hurried in the direction of the explosion, nobody seems to have had the presence of mind enough to look for the bandits' car. Everybody was afraid to attempt to leave from the front of the bank for fear of being shot down by the bandits. No effort was made to stop them as they departed and everybody was afraid to follow them.

A few days later, the *Joplin Globe* ran an eyewitness account of the running gun battle in its coverage of the robbery.

...A vivid description of the robbery was furnished by Dr. R. V. Thompson, who heard the explosions while he was on his way to catch an early train for Kansas City. "I never returned to my office, instead I got my revolver and went to the post office doorway opposite the bank," Dr. Thompson said. "Several roomers sleeping in the second story of the bank building started downstairs, but were held back by one of the robbers who posted himself at the foot of the stairs and threatened to shoot. It was almost impossible to see the robbers because they had put out the streetlights at the corner."

The article went on to say that:

...Practically the entire population whose number was swelled by curious visitors from nearby towns, went through the building today to glimpse, the yawning doors of the safe and vault and to examine the shattered plate glass windows. ...Members of the bandit gang are believed to have been novices at the safe blowing game. Enough nitroglycerin to blow half a dozen safes was used, according to members of the sheriff's force. ...How Chamberlain, the night marshal, escaped death from the explosion is a mystery. Chamberlain believes that he was freed of his bonds by the detonation in some way but doesn't remember clearly when he was liberated. While the bandits were looting the safe and the vault he reached for his revolver and opened fire. He was silenced by a charge from a shotgun, which wounded him in the head and back.

The *Gallatin Democrat* reported that someone had squealed on the Newtons' plans by saying,

> ... (The robbery) was not entirely unexpected by bank or city officials, for a tip was received here some two months ago that plans had been made for a robbery here. In fact, the bankers were rather suspecting one at the time the attempt was made to rob the Winston bank several weeks ago and special precautions were taken. Arms had been stored in banks and nearby stores for use especially in case of a daylight robbery.

Comparing Willis' account of the Gallatin robbery with the various newspaper accounts, it is obvious that more people were wounded in the gun battle and that the Newton Gang was very lucky to have made it out alive. Apparently, the body of the one casualty of the firefight, "Des Moines Billy," was never discovered.

New Braunfels, Texas

After living the high life in San Antonio for a few weeks Willis decided he was going to pull off a daylight stick-up of the New Braunfels State Bank. New Braunfels was a bustling German community about 40 miles north of San Antonio and it is the county seat of Comal County. It had two major banks at the time.

> *"I went over there and watched the State Bank around noon time a couple of times and seen that they hardly had any customers walk in around noon. Them Germans like to eat a big lunch. With nobody coming in, it would be a piece of cake. As you walked in, there was a guy sitting in a chair and all you had to do was jump over that little fence, you was in behind there with him.*

> *"We was driving a big Buick and we got there just before noon. I told them, 'Now little after twelve, we will drive right up there. Joe, you stay behind the wheel, and Doc you stay in the car too. Don't you get out unless*

somebody gives us trouble or if somebody comes into the bank. Then you jump out and follow them on in.'

"I took Jess with me and let him go in first with me coming right behind. I told him to pull out a $20 bill and walk up to the counter like he wanted change. Soon as he reached the counter I jumped over this little fence and I was in behind them—there was four or five people in there. I had a big .44 on them and I talked real tough to them, trying to scare the hell out of them. 'We're robbing this bank, lay down here, now!' They done like I said and I lined them up on the floor.

"While I was inside the bank Joe and Doc seen a man come from the courthouse and looked like he was headed for the bank. Just as the man went in the door Doc stuck a gun in his back and walked him on in while Joe stayed with the car. I had filled a flour sack with cash and Liberty bonds when Doc marched the man over to the rest of us. He was an ex-Texas Ranger that worked at the bank that was coming back from lunch. When he opened the door, he seen what was happening. He started to turn but Doc pushed him in the bank with a pistol and said, 'Get on in there.' We brought him back around the counter and had him lay down with the rest of them."

Then Willis gave the money sack to Doc and told him to return to the car while he went over the cash register. While stuffing cash into another sack, he spotted a locked tin box. Remembering that another gang had robbed a bank in Houston where they found a locked tin box that contained over $60,000 in Liberty bonds, Willis grabbed the box and headed out the bank door.

"Jess and me come out of the bank, walked over to the car, and I told Joe, 'Go along.' He drove a few blocks, made some wrong turns and finally we left town. We took our time driving out into the country, not driving fast.

"The people in the bank did as I told them for about 15 minutes and then somebody grabbed a Winchester and ran out and shot it in the air hollering, 'Robbery! Robbery!'

"We went about four miles out then turned down a little road and went about two miles more. We came to the spot we had planned out and I opened the gate and we drove in. I had cut brush all ready and used it to cover up car tracks. We run the car into that brush with the top down and then covered it all with cedar limbs. We got out all of our money, crossed the road, and went up a little hill. Them cedars were thick and you couldn't see nothing, but we could see cars coming up and down the road."

When they were well hidden, they counted out the cash in the sack and then opened the tin box. To Willis' chagrin, the box only contained loan notes—worthless. They had just finished stuffing all of the cash in the tin box when they heard airplanes overhead.

"Directly, here come the airplanes but they never spotted us hidden in them cedars. We ate some food we had put away and laid around there until about two o'clock that night and the cars finally stopped driving up and down the road.

"At daylight, we come out of there and cut across a little road until we got to the road that went into San Antonio. We drove until we come across the first streetcar line and I got out. A little farther Doc got out and then later Jess got out and took a street car down to the Menger Hotel. Joe took the car and planted it 'cause we had stolen it.

"Before I got out of the car, we had stopped and I hid everything in the tin box, including our pistols. We didn't want to take the stuff with us, in case we got caught. We got about $20,000 in cash and $80,000 in Liberty and Victory bonds. The paper said we got a whole lot more

but that's all we got. If they said they lost more than that, then I damn well know it was the employees or somebody else at the bank that took it. When a bank's been robbed, why they can take cash, bonds, or gold out themselves and say it was taken in the robbery. I saw that happen over and over again."

The next day, Willis took the car and retrieved the cash and bonds. Then, returning to San Antonio, he packed the loot in his wife's suitcase and put her on a train to New Orleans.

"...I drove over there in another car and met her at a restaurant. Then we got on a Illinois Central passenger train headed for Chicago that night.

"We checked into the Blackstone Hotel in Chicago and I started peddling the bonds. About a week later I got a hold of my brothers and told them to come on up. I got ninety cents on the dollar for the bonds and I gave everybody their share—a five-way split. My wife had a safe deposit box where she kept our money along with Joe's money."

This brazen daylight robbery caught the attention of all the newspapers across Texas. The best account appeared in the *New Braunfels Herald Zeitung* on March 16, 1922. Written in German, it translates into:

$100,000 Bank Robbery in New Braunfels

A bold bank robbery took place here Friday between twelve and one o'clock noon. Two robbers, of whom one had tied a handkerchief over the lower part of his face and the other was not masked, entered the new Braunfels State Bank, ordered the bank personnel present at the moment, with revolvers pointed threateningly at them, to lie face down, flat on the floor, pulled the roller shades down and took gold, paper money, bonds and other securities to the total sum of over $100,000, ordered the bank personnel into the vault, shut the vault door, and left in an automobile in which two other bandits were sitting.

As soon as the bank personnel could free themselves from their prison they rushed out and gave the panic alarm in front of the bank, the fire alarm bell was rung, and preparations were begun to follow the robbers, that, however, up to now have brought no results.

All officers in West Texas are trying to find tracks of the robbers for the arrest and conviction of whom rewards totaling $6,000 have been set out.

...A stranger with his wife who drew suspicion on themselves were arrested, however, seemingly evidence could not be proven that they had connections with a gang of robbers.

During the search and surrounding areas the San Antonio Air Police for the first time had an opportunity to take part in the search for the criminals with three airplanes.

It was about 12:25 o'clock when a man entered the bank, pointed a revolver at the president of the bank, Mr. F. G. Bloomberg, and ordered him to quickly hold up his hands.

At the same time a second bandit jumped over the banister in front of the president's desk and, threatening them with a revolver, gave similar orders to Cashier R. E. Kloepper, Assistant Cashier A. R. Ludwig, and Bookkeeper Clarence Wetzel.

The robbers then ordered all to lie face down, flat on the floor, and as one of the robbers with a cocked revolver watched that no one moved, the other robber grabbed money and security papers from the drawers and the vault.

Without suspecting anything wrong, Bookkeeper Harold Adams, at that time returned from a mission in town, as he entered the bank was followed by a third member of the bandits, who with drawn revolver, ordered him to also lie down on the floor.

After the robbers had grabbed the money and valuable papers, they drove the five named into the vault and closed the door.

After some five minutes of effort the imprisoned succeeded in opening the vault door and gave alarm immediately.

...The automobile used by the bandits is said to be a Buick Six. At the time the robbery was going on in the bank, City Marshal Ed Moeller in passing saw the car with two occupants, in front of the bank. But there was nothing to call suspicion that there was anything out of the ordinary going on inside the bank.

One of the robbers wore a handkerchief tied over his mouth, the others were unmasked. They were smoothly shaven and were young men, probably 25 to 35 years old.

In a short time, city and county officers and also Rangers from a 100-mile surrounding area were actively in search of, and seeking, if possible, to stop and arrest the fleeing robbers. Three planes constantly flew back and forth over the territory through which their car would have to travel.

...It was reported that the robbers were hiding in the Forshage pasture between Bracken and Bulverde, and an assumption seems to be borne out that from there they were trying to get to San Antonio. The area has many caves, ravines and thickets as if made for just such a place of refuge.

Sheriff Nowotny, Deputy Marshal Meredith and some 50 armed volunteers went there and thoroughly searched every nook; but after all nothing was found.

...It is believed that the robbery was by professionals who came from the big cities in the north to spend the winter in the south, and that possibly could be the same who recently attempted to rob the First National Bank of New Braunfels.

This is a translation of the German version of the newspaper. The wording is complicated because of the translation. It is interesting to note that while other newspaper accounts varied in the amount taken the German version of the story gives you the exact amount of money stolen during the robbery. A prime example of German exactness.

Willis said the one wearing "a handkerchief over the lower part of his face" was Doc and he told his brother to take it off his head when they left the bank.

"We didn't wear masks, I had pair dark glasses on and that was all. I never did get recognized. If you go in there with masks, people see a masked man and they know you're robbing the bank. If you haven't got a mask on, just walk along like anybody else and act normal, they won't know what you're doing."

Just as he had told his brothers, the bank's money was insured. There was an Associated Press Report dated March 10, 1922, which read:

Has $100,000 Insurance

AUSTIN, Texas—The robbing of the New Braunfels State Bank of approximately $100,000 in money and bonds will not affect its business operation, T. T. Brady Jr., deputy banking commissioner, said today after a telephone conversation with officials of the bank. The officials said they had sufficient funds to meet all demands, according to Mr. Priddy: also that the bank had $100,000 burglar insurance. It is a guaranteed fund bank.

Another Associated Press Report dated March 10, 1922, gave an "enhanced" version of the story:

Officers Searched Hills for $100,000 Loot And Robbers
$18,622 Cash Taken From New Braunfels Bank at Noon Hour.

AUSTIN, Texas. March 10.—A man who officers say gives his name as R. E. McGrew of Kansas City, claims to be a professional gambler, is being held in the Comal County jail tonight for investigation in connection with the robbery of the New Braunfels State Bank today. He was arrested by the Comal County Sheriff.

Every available officer in this section of the state and a band of 150 New Braunfels citizens armed with rifles and shotguns were searching last night for some trace of five bandits who yesterday at noon held up five officials and employees of the New Braunfels State Bank and escaped in an automobile with more than $100,000 in cash, Liberty Bonds and bonds of Comal County and the city of New Braunfels.

Aerial police from San Antonio in three planes joined in the search yesterday afternoon. The amount of the loot was at first reported to be $70,000, but a re-check last night by F. G. Bloomberg, president of the bank, showed it was missing $18,622 in gold and currency and $83,000 in bonds. The bonds included $55,000 in five Liberty Loan issues, $26,200 in County and city bonds and $1800 in War Savings Stamps.

Though numerous reports have been received from persons claiming to have seen automobiles answering the description of the bandit's car, officers reported no definite clue up to the late hour last night. A man and woman, however, are being detained at New Braunfels and were questioned in an effort to locate some confederate of the band.

The fire alarm was sounded at New Braunfels late yesterday afternoon and a large number of citizens responded with officers to join in the search. The 150 men were divided into groups and were combing the woods and hills about the town last night.

F. G. Bloomberg, president of the bank, who was one of the five held up and locked in the vault, told the story of his adventure last night.

"It was about 12:25 o'clock," he said, "when a man appeared at the cashier's window with a gun leveled on me and commanded me to 'stick 'em up.' I was talking to the cashier and when the man first spoke I looked up at him and laughed, not realizing the situation. He commanded me again to 'stick 'em up and be quick about it.' I complied.

In the meantime another man had rushed by the railing and held up cashier R.E. Kloepper, assistant cashier Albert Ludwig and Clarence Wetzel, a bookkeeper.

The two men then compelled us to lie on the floor face down. One of them went through the vault and cash drawer, while the second kept us covered.

In the meantime Harold Adams, a bookkeeper, who had been on an errand, returned and as he entered the door was covered by a third man and compelled to join us on the floor.

When the men had got the money and bonds they pushed all five of us into the vault and locked the door. It took me about 5 min. to work on it and spread the alarm.

...Aerial police with three planes from San Antonio were circling the country about the little towns throughout the afternoon. Their search extended over several hundred miles above every road leading out of town. It is the first important case that has brought out the aerial police, who were commissioned several weeks ago by Mayor Black.

...Upon his return last night, Chief Martin said he had questioned a man and a woman detained in New Braunfels. The chief said he was informed that four men had driven up in front of the bank Thursday afternoon and that one of the men had got out of the car and looked the bank building over. The woman, he said had gone to San Antonio in an automobile just after the robbery.

"It was learned," Chief Martin, said, "that the woman had inquired of the station agent at the depot in New Braunfels if there was a train leaving soon—going either way. After learning that there would be no train she took the jitney line and came to San Antonio, the officers were told. She went back to New Braunfels after six o'clock yesterday afternoon."

The man told the officers he was an oil worker from Oklahoma. Several keys were found on his person.

One of the clues being investigated by San Antonio officers is the report of a man who arrived here about eight o'clock last night from Bandera.

This man said he had seen a Buick automobile containing three men driving in the direction of San Antonio on the Bandera Road that the car had followed him for a distance of about 10 miles and turned off the main road at a point near Spring Creek, 35 miles northwest of here.

An eyewitness account of the robbery appeared in the *New Braunfels Herald* (the English version) a week later:

Mrs. Fred Withem, the cashier of the M. K. & T. Railroad walked into the bank at noon to make a $5,000 deposit. As she left the bank, she heard a strange hissing noise.

She looked back to see a Buick touring car driving slowly and then coming to a stop quite a distance from the curb, not like the other cars that park head-in.

She noticed five men getting out of the car and walking back toward the bank. About 10 min. later, while she was sitting down to eat dinner, she recalls, "the shot was fired announcing the robbery."

Next door, Emil Marion at the Plaza Hotel restaurant said that just after noon, two men came in and ordered two cups of coffee. He noticed that they had handkerchiefs hanging around the lower part of their faces but didn't think they looked like masks.

Perhaps they had been "riding in the wind." They gave him two bits ($.25) and he had to go out to get change.

On his way back, he heard a whistle and when he

got back into the restaurant, the men were gone, but the coffee had not been tasted.

Meanwhile, inside the bank, cashier Kloepper had just returned before Mrs. Withem left. President Bloomberg was counting her deposit. Assistant cashier Ludwig and bookkeeper Clarence Wetzel were also there. When Bloomberg looked up, a man wearing sunglasses stuck a gun in his face and demanded that they all hold their hands up.

A second armed man jumped the railing and ordered all employees to lie on the floor while the robbers collected the loot.

The other bookkeeper, Harold Adams, came back to the bank at this time and one of the men poked a gun against his chest.

The robbers completed the robbery and all of the bank employees were marched into the vault. The robbers thought they were secure, but the bankers got out immediately through "a little device recently installed" and the alarm was given.

The robbers got away in the Buick.

When the fire alarm was given, a crowd gathered outside the bank thinking it was a fire, but when they found out it was a robbery, there was "some confusion for about five minutes"

Available cars loaded with heavily armed local men left on the route they thought the robbers had taken across the bridge at Landa Park toward the hills.

Another eyewitness to the robbery was Harold Adams, the ex-Texas Ranger, who was shoved inside by Doc Newton. He later recalled:

"I was coming back from lunch a little early when I saw this car parked in front of the bank. I noticed two things out of the way about it, but didn't think much about this at the time.

One thing, the car was parked headed north in the wrong direction for traffic, and it was about 10 feet from the curb.

"As I passed I saw a man sitting in the backseat, and the driver was in the front. As I started toward the bank door the driver got out and followed me in. As I entered the bank he said to me, 'Get down on your belly!'

"They worked fast and they were professionals. I could see a man back in the vault stuffing things into a suitcase. Another came out and was picking up money and papers in the cashier cages. We had the note box out, and they picked that up. They told us to get back inside the vault and lay down. They said to stay there. They shut the door and left.

"The outside door to the vault didn't shut properly, so the men in the vault worked through the steel bars of the daytime door and got that door open.

"One of the officers of the bank, R.E. Kloepper, cashier, had an old Springfield rifle at the bank so he grabbed it, ran out into the street, aimed in the air and shot. The ammunition must have been old for it didn't make a lot of noise.

"Well, it didn't take long for the town to get into action. In a few minutes at least 1,000 people, alarmed by the fire bell's ringing (the fire bell hung on a standard in the back of the courthouse), were crowded in front of the bank on the plaza.

"The bandit car ran north out of the plaza, went down a couple of blocks, turned and came back after a while and went out the road leading west under the railroad and out past Landa Park.

"...Ranger Capt. Frank Hamer from Austin came with a posse, and during that afternoon the road sang with the whine of tires in the greatest manhunt of the era of the coming age of the automobiles.

"...I got kidded a good deal about the robbery. Before I went to work for the bank I was a Ranger, and people thought it was mighty funny that a former Ranger walked right into the middle of the bank robbery and had to lie down, like all the rest.

"That afternoon, this part of Texas was having a field day. I can still remember the fast ride over the Austin Post Road and the stories repeated as excited officers returned to the plaza to report on forays toward Fredericksburg, San Marcos, and other points where mysterious, fast driving cars had been seen.

"The bandits, however, had well-laid plans. After snaking out of New Braunfels in a manner to throw off pursuers, they went west, turned down a side road toward Bulverde, and took another side road, which they had patrolled for two weeks to ensure few people ever used it.

"Then they went to a pasture, divided the loot (which contained $4,000 in gold,) and burned the checks and contents of the note box.

"Of course, everything was covered by insurance. All that was left out in the Forshage pasture where the robbers divided the loot was a wooden cash box and a five dollar gold piece they had dropped."

Harold Adams—Texas Ranger and later as a clerk in the New Braunfels
State Bank.

So, with all the newspaper coverage, eyewitness accounts, sheriffs' posses, and the Texas Ranger Captain Frank Hamer (who tracked down Bonnie and Clyde) scouring the countryside, Willis Newton and his brothers were never prosecuted for the bank robbery and they spent every dime of the $100,000 loot.

Toronto Currency Clearing House Robbery

After venturing into the oil drilling business in Oklahoma, Willis and his brothers hit a series of dry holes and lost most of what they had saved from their robberies. With a small amount of cash reserves Willis traveled to Toronto, Canada, in July of 1923.

> *"One day while I was walking round in Toronto I seen two guys pass by me carrying a big old bag, one on each side. Then I spied two more men across the street doing the same thing. Pretty soon I seen more men lugging heavy sacks up the street. It was around eight o'clock in the morning. So I watched them until they went into a big bank.*

> *"Then, while I was standing there a dozen or so come out of the bank carrying bags of money—two on each side of the bag. After walking a few blocks some of the men would split off and head in a different directions.*

> *"This is where Toronto has all of its banks, at least 10 or better. In them days every bank had its own money, with its own name on it so at the end of the day they sent all their money to a clearing house where they separated it up.*

> *"Then come the next morning, each bank sent out guards and got its currency back in them heavy bags."*

Willis could not believe his eyes, bank money being toted up the street by two men carrying a bag with a single guard trailing behind with no shotguns. "They only had them little short bulldog pistols that couldn't hit nothing past ten feet."

He immediately sent for his brothers and they spent several days watching the couriers' routine. After deciding the job was doable they bought an automatic shotgun and sawed eight inches off the barrel.

Willis then spotted a Big Six Studebaker with the keys in the ignition and within minutes had started the car and driven it to a rented garage about six block away. They were set.

"The plan was that we would pull out right behind the bagmen after they had crossed in front of the car. I got in front and Joe drove the car, with Jess and Doc in the back. I had a shotgun under my coat and a long-barreled pistol in my pocket.

"When the men with bags come across the front of the car, I came out with that shotgun and I says, 'Give me that bag!'

"But hell no, they wouldn't give it up. So after yanking on it as hard as I could I finally decided to use the shotgun and riddled a nearby telephone pole. I thought that would scare them, but that didn't work a bit.

"Then one of them jumped on me. I went to shoot the shotgun at his feet but the damned thing was jammed. I pulled and pulled on the bolt but it wouldn't budge.

"So I pulled out my pistol with the guy hanging on my back but the hammer got caught in the coat lining so I had to drop the shotgun to get it out.

"One of the men grabbed it and come at me. I told him, 'Drop that gun!' Damned if he wasn't going to shoot me with that shotgun—jammed or not.

"I didn't have a choice so I plugged him high on the right side.

"I grabbed that bag, and when I did I seen Doc was wrestling with another messenger over his bag. The guard pulled his bulldog pistol and Doc had to shoot him.

"I went around the car and the other messengers had run off down an alley carrying three or four of them money bags. They had shed from Jess and Doc who were hot on their trail.

"So I threw my bag into the car where Joe was sitting. Then before I know it, an old sedan come roaring up that was full of them bank messengers and they run right at me.

"A guy on the passenger side run his window down and was leveling his pistol on me when I shot through his door and caught him in the groin. His door flew open and his pistol rolled out at my feet as he high-tailed it away

"Doc and Jess come running up and pitched in one bag— that's all they got."

As this Canadian comedy of errors continued it took on more of a Keystone Cops tone when things started raining down on the Newtons and the bank men.

"Crap, it was like a hailstorm, them people throwing things out of windows up above us. They was throwing chairs, bottles, ashtrays, boxes—anything they could get out the windows right on top of us.

"I hollered to Jess and Doc, 'Get in the car and let's go!' Then I told Joe, 'Get the hell out of here!' and he took off."

As Joe gunned the car away, a guard was running behind, shooting his pistol in the air. They slowed to make a turn and then ran into heavy traffic with the man hot on their trail. After a few yards the man began to gain on them running down the sidewalk hollering at the Newtons.

Joe spotted a big plate glass window on a storefront coming up in

80

front of the running man. He leveled his shotgun on the window and hit it dead center. The window exploded, sending pieces of glass in every direction.

Startled, the man came to an abrupt halt and gave up the chase.

"How we ever got away, I'll never know. We hit a main street and cut in between some other cars and just kept going.

"There was big a policeman standing there directing traffic. Just as we run up there and I was fixing to jump out and throw down on him with my pistol but he stuck out his hand to stop the other cars and told us to come on!

"Would you believe that, he didn't know what we had done and he turned the traffic the other way and stopped the bank men behind us.

"About two blocks up there was two policemen directing traffic on the right. The traffic wasn't so heavy so Joe asked me if I wanted him to stop. I looked it over and said, 'No. When you get there don't go but pull out on the left of him and I'll holler at him.'

"We got there and Joe pulls out by the man, and I waved my arm at him and bless Pat, if he didn't let us go around him!

"After that we monkeyed around a few streets and made it to our garage. Soon as the car stopped we was out shutting the door and scattering up the street."

Toronto crowds gather at the location where the Newton brothers held up
bank messengers carrying money bags from the Toronto clearing house.

Willis headed to another garage where he had a car hidden. Jess
took a streetcar back to their hotel while Joe and Doc casually walked
down to a movie theater and spent the next three hours watching
movies. Later, they left the theater, separated, and then went back to
their separate rooms at a high-class hotel.

> *"I had a car parked near there because I had just come
> up that morning from Hamilton where I was staying with
> my wife in a hotel. So, calm as you please, I got into my
> car and drove back over there. By the time I got to
> Hamilton you should have seen them people—everybody
> was talking about the robbery. Damn, what a
> commotion!"*

The sensational day-light hold up and running gun battle lit up the
news wires on both sides of the Canadian border. Bold splash
headlines filled the newspapers—often blurring the facts and

sometimes jumping to erroneous conclusions. The *Moberly Weekly Monitor* on July 26, 1923 was one of the early accounts:

Bandits Kill Bank Messenger

Toronto, July 24—Six bandits in a motor car today fired a volley into a crowd of three bank messengers at King and Young streets, one of the city's busiest corners, and fled with pouches believed to have contained thousands of dollars. First reports received by the police said one man had been killed and two wounded, perhaps mortally.

Then the *Manitoba Free Press* hit the newsstands with an enhanced version of the story (pay attention to the street names).

Toronto Bank Robbery Loss Put at $125,000.
Three Messengers Seriously Wounded but
Recovery of All Expected.
No Trace of Bandits
When Last Seen Were Heading Westward,
Apparently to Hamilton Highway.

Toronto—July 24.—At a late hour tonight the gang of bandits who this morning staged a sensational holdup in the heart of the Toronto business section, and fled with $125,000 in currency, after shooting down three bank messengers and another man who went to their assistance, was still at large, while officers of the law putting forth every effort to find traces of them.

The robbers made their escape in a large car, which had been stolen from a resident of East Toronto late Saturday night. Police arrived on the scene just as the robbers were departing and took up the chase, but were outdistanced by the bandit's car after traveling about two miles.

When last seen by the police, the bandits were heading westward apparently toward the Hamilton Highway. Speed patrol officers tried to intercept a speeding car a short distance from the city on the highway during the afternoon and it is believed to have contained the fleeing bandits.

A warning was flashed from Toronto in all directions and a carload of police armed with rifles went west on Hamilton to look for the bandits, but they were not seen.

Two large bags were seized by the bandits, while one messenger fled from a nearby office with a pouch containing $100,000 in gold. Some of the messengers used their revolvers but their fire was ineffective, although spectators who watched the battle from the windows said one of the bandits was wounded and the others had to help him to the car. The exchange of shots continued but the bandits car vanished around the nearest corner with bullets flying after it.

The bank messengers were apprehended on their way from the clearinghouse to their several banks. The intersection of Jordan and Melinda streets was the point for the attack. Jordan is a one-way street for automobiles and very narrow. It is believed that an armed bandit occupied each corner of the intersection.

Leading the march of the messengers were the uniformed men of the Sterling Bank of Canada and the bank of Nova Scotia. The cash of the latter bank was contained in two bags, all that of the Sterling Bank was in one.

As they approached the corner, the men from the four corners closed in on them. Two of them placed sawed-off shotguns against the bodies of the two messengers and at the same time grabbed for the bags. These were thrown by the bandits into their car, which stood at the curb.

By this time the other messengers riding in a car, approached the intersection and one of them, James Harris, pulled a revolver from a companion's pocket and opened fire on the robbers.

A robber in shirt sleeves was then noticed standing in the center of the intersection directing operations while another stood near the car. All were armed. After firing two shots from his car, Harris continued shooting, but soon fell when a bullet pierced his stomach. Even after being shot he raised himself on his elbow and emptied his revolver at the bandits.

A. F. Duck of the Union Bank was just getting his revolver out for action when he fell from one of the bandit's bullets.

Alan Lard, elevator man at the McMillian building, engaged in a hand-to-hand struggle with one of the bandits, even after three shots were fired at him. He grappled with the bandit and caught his gun. They wrestled in the middle of the street. Lard finally got the gun, and raising himself up, smashed the bandit on the head. The robber then whipped a revolver from a side pocket and opened fire. A shot struck Lord in the knee. He dropped his gun and ran in a zigzag course from the scene. Several shots flew about him and he escaped further injury.

By this time the bandits had made their way to the big automobile standing on Jordan Street. The leader of the bandits got all his pals safely into the automobile and then gave the word to "go."

City policeman have learned that the bandits stole the license number of their automobile from a parked car in North Toronto this morning. The police have also learned that the car was stolen on July 23. "It will be very hard to catch the men because we don't have much of a description of them," declared General Williams of the provincial police. "About all the information we have is that one of the men was tall and that they were all foreign looking."

The police have a clue in the form of a sawed-off shotgun, which the bandits threw from the automobile just before it started. This gun may have valuable fingerprints on it. They also found several shotgun shells loaded with bird shot and buckshot.

Then later, the *Manitoba Free Press* reported on July 30:

Car Used by Toronto Bank Bandits Found Discovered In Isolated Barn On Farm About 10 Miles North East of the City.

Number of Checks Left.
Bloodstains In Stolen Bag Found In Car Prove One of Robbers Wounded.

Toronto. July 25—One definite step toward a solution of the $82,000 Toronto bank robbery mystery; which had its inception when six unknown desperados held up bank messengers at Jordan and Melinda streets on Tuesday morning last, came tonight when Toronto police recovered the robbers' car in an isolated barn, about 10 miles north east of Toronto city limits.

The car was found by three Toronto men, as they were being shown over the farm. Examination of the car revealed two of the stolen bags, one of which was bloodstained on the inside, indicating that, as rumor had it, one of the bandits was wounded in the running fight with the messengers. The bags also contained a large number of bank checks, all from the Sterling Bank and the Bank of Nova Scotia.

The car also showed bullet holes in several places.

By the time Willis got back to the hotel in Hamilton, his wife was frantically trying to find out which of the gang had been injured.

"They had a big black board at the hotel and they put up that the robbers got so much money and there was four of them and one was captured.

"Louise saw the message and went to pieces when I come sashaying in. She thought sure that I had been shot and taken captive. She always was a nervous sort."

Before the getaway car was found by authorities, Willis and his brothers had gone back to the garage and retrieved the stolen money.

"I got one bag and Doc got one bag and that was all. Doc got $68,000 in his, and I got $12,000 in mine. Jess didn't get anything. We drove the car and the money out into the country about 30 miles.

"Then we took a sharp-nose shovel, made a good hole, and buried the money. Covered it up nice and neat and them we come on back to Toronto."

The following day the Newtons went back and retrieved the hidden money from the robbery. They used some cotton ducking material to make homemade money belts, which they strapped to their torsos like vests. After donning their clothes and coats they calmly caught a ferry going to Niagara Falls and then later traveled by train to Chicago.

"We had a fence there that could turn the Canadian into American money if you give him 10 cents on the dollar. I went and looked up the guy and he said that he had to take it to Detroit to turn the money. So me and him went to Detroit and he turned it all for me."

Tab & Spencer, Indiana

After "monkeying around" in Chicago for a few weeks enjoying the best hotels and restaurants, movies and professional baseball games, Willis met with a man that promised him two easy scores in Tab and two banks in Spencer, Indiana. Bringing the man along as a partner, the gang drove to Tab.

When they arrived in Tab they found that one of the banks had closed—a common occurrence during the troubled economic times of the Twenties. Hitting the other bank seemed simple enough but had a violent ending.

"So, we went up there to that bank and I told them, 'I'll stay outside with this other guy while you boys go in there and blow it.' They took off up stairs to the bank.

"There weren't no night watchman or anybody around so I told this guy with us, 'Stand over there behind them posts so nobody upstairs can see you.' I went outside and

stood in the dark where I could see anybody coming.

"I'll be swan if that idiot didn't come out and stand there where anybody could spot him; he just stood there. Well they set off a shot and knocked off the first door. While they was setting up the next shot, somebody raised up a window, seen that guy standing there and cut down on him with a .22 automatic. One of the shots caught him right in the back. Damned if he didn't drop his shotgun and the thing went off! Blew out a plate glass window right in front of me! I hollered at him, 'What the hell is a matter?' He said, 'I'm shot!'

"He come limping over to me and I called for the boys to give up on the safe. 'It'll take us over an hour and this boy's in bad shape. We've got to get him to a doctor.'

"I knowed a guy over in Chicago that could get us a doctor so we took him there and he later died. Damn shame!"

Shortly after midnight on November 6, 1923, the Newton boys rolled into Spencer, Indiana riding in a new Big Six Studebaker. Willis had it planned like the Hondo job by hitting two banks in one night. Since they had lost their tipster in the botched Tab job there were only four of them that night.

"Jess and me went to the lower bank and I sent Joe and Doc over the other bank on the corner. It had one of them big old Packer safes that sat on the floor so it was easy to shoot. I took the other one because it had one of them new drum doors on its vault. That door is 10 inches thick and not once has one of them ever been shot before or since but I done it.

"I took a piece of my case knife and hammered at it until I got a little opening. That's all I needed, I took my soap and made a cup and poured about an ounce of grease in

there. I pushed a cap in there and used a 20 second string. I lit the string and just stepped out the front door. I barely got around the corner when Blam, she went!

"It was a hell of a shot but it only made a small gap in the door. That's all I needed so I put me another soap cup around it and poured about eight ounces of grease. I lit the string on that sucker and boy, what a blast! That big vault door come flying off, hit the floor and went straight on down to the basement. Damn!

"The blast took out all of the windows from where we was to where Joe and Doc was working on the other bank. When I looked in there was the vault standing wide-open. So I went in there and found a round safe inside that you couldn't shoot. I thought I would give it a try so I turned the crank and like we'd seen in other banks, it wasn't locked! They must' a thought, hell, no one can come through the vault door so there was no need to lock the little safe but I done it.

"I got about $8,000 in cash out of that safe and come on out of the bank. Joe and Doc was still shooting the safe down at the other bank.

"We went down there and we come across the old night hack that was standing over at the courthouse. He wanted to know what we were doing.

"I told him, 'We're going to rob these banks.' Then we tied him up on a stool and set him out where we could see him in front of the courthouse. About that time a telephone man come running up and we latched on to him.

"Joe come up from the other bank and we went down a back alley. You could hear people hollering and shooting guns in every direction, but we got to our car and we *could still see that the old man sitting there on that chair under the courthouse light.*

"We drove over to this to this old man's farm house and laid up there for a few days. He was just a poor dirt farmer, so we gave him about $1000 in hard currency. I guess we got $35,000-$40,000 anyway, from the two banks.

"After that we come on back to Chicago. Then we went on back down to Texas, just before deer hunting season that winter."

Joe Newton driving a Big Six Studebaker.

Needless to say the newspapers filled up front pages with the accounts of the two-bank heist. The *Livingston Daily Sun* on November 7 ran the headline:

**Large Band of Robbers Blow Two Indiana Banks
14 to 20 Men in Party, Which Traveled In Four
Automobiles.**

Spencer, Indiana. November 6—A band of
robbers variously estimated in number between
14 and 20 men robbed two banks here early
today of approximately $15,000 and wounded
two citizens.

Traveling in four automobiles, the robbers first
isolated the town, cutting all telephone and
telegraph lines, and then posted guards to
prevent interruption while they blew open both
bank vaults.

The bandits remained in town over an hour and
in gaining access to the banks vaults, used
several explosive charges, almost wrecking one
of the buildings.

The banks entered were the National Bank of
Spencer and the Exchange Bank.

The *Linton Daily Citizen* article followed on the theory that the
banks were hit by a small army of amateur bank burglars—with
estimates as high as twenty men.

**Two Spencer Banks Robbed Today
Spectacular and Unusual Double Bank Raid Is
Made
Two Spencer Citizens Shot by Fleeing Robbers As
Crowd Gathers.
Night Watchman Is Bound and Gagged
All Wires Were Cut and Communication Was Not
Reestablished until Late Today**

Spencer, Indiana. November 6.—Between 12,000
and $15,000 was obtained by bandits here early
today who dissented on this city, stationed
guards and cut light and communication wires,
while they robbed the First National and
Exchange State Banks.

Two men, J.E. Barge, a baker, and Frank Gray,
furniture dealer, were wounded, and night
watchman Vaughn was bound, gagged and
locked in the city building.

Officials of the Exchange Bank said it appeared
that $7000 had been taken; all officials of the
First National Bank were unable to estimate
accurately the amount taken, as safety deposit

boxes were looted as well as the vault.

Dynamite charges were used at both institutions and the fixtures of the banks were wrecked.

It was impossible to get telephone or telegraph connection with Spencer, until late this afternoon.

The story of the spectacular double robbery and shooting, which plunged this erstwhile quiet town into a fervor of excitement such as was never known, is relayed by a messenger sent by the International News Service correspondent.

When the last message came through it was thought that none of the men wounded were fatally hurt, though it may develop that one or more of them are.

The promiscuous shooting in the early hours of the morning and the noise of the several dynamite explosions in the two banks drew numbers of citizen up town and many came armed, joining the fusillade of shots, which followed the robbers as they ran for their automobile.

There are various estimates as to the number of men in the robbery gang there were three or four cars of them and estimates of the number of robbers run as high as eighteen to twenty, but it appears that from a the best available stories that there were but five.—one man remained in the car, the engine of which was kept running and the two men are said to have visited each bank assignments tenuously.

It may be found, and probably will, that more than five men took part in this unusual double robbery.

A large posse of men in cars all heavily armed was at once organized and followed the fleeing bandit car, which is said to have gone south and across the river bridge in the direction of Bloomington.

...The very size of the party and the rather crude way in which the vaults were shot open lead officers to believe that the job was done by daring amateurs rather than by expert safecrackers.

The next day the *Connersville News–Examiner* took a different tack—that the robbery was a well-planned operation by a large gang of highly skilled safe men.

No Trace Found of Bank Bandits
24 Hour Search without Results in Spencer Case
Robbery Carefully Planned

Spencer, Indiana November 7—Members of the bandit gang of fifteen or twenty men who raided Spencer Monday night and looted the Exchange National Bank and the Spencer National Bank of $13,000 had apparently made good their getaway today.

Twenty-four hours of searching by sheriffs and police throughout all of northern Indiana failed to reveal a single trace of the high-powered motorcars, which sped away in the light of early dawn after the robbery.

...The robbery was perhaps the most carefully planned in the history of the state. Spencer was completely isolated from surrounding communities when the robbers cut telephone and telegraph wires.

Sentries armed with sawed-off shotguns stood at the four corners of the public square, and sharpshooters trained their guns on the bank fronts from adjoining buildings while two details of safecrackers blew the bank vaults.

The bandits were gone an hour or two before the alarm reached the neighboring towns and an organize search was started.

It was believed they had had time to reach Indianapolis or got well under way to some other large city before the search was started.

The two men shot by the bandits were only slightly wounded. Both banks were covered by insurance against losses from burglary.

As the newspaper article reported—with all the eyewitnesses and massive search parties, the Newton gang of four men, driving a single Studebaker, looted both banks and got away without a trace. They were never prosecuted for the two-bank heist. Willis and his brothers casually returned to Texas to concentrate on hunting whitetail deer around Uvalde. And plan their next bank job.

San Marcos, Texas

By January 4, 1924, Willis and his brothers had killed all the deer they wanted and it was time to get back to what they did best—stealing money from "them other thieves." They had driven up to San Marcos earlier to lay out their plans for hitting the State Bank and Trust Company. The bank lay opposite the courthouse on a corner. Willis figured the roads out of San Marcos were too risky so the brothers selected a hide-out spot about three miles out of town just off the highway to San Antonio. They had driven a man over to the spot and instructed him to meet them there at an appointed time the next night after the robbery. While they were there they hid some knapsacks and provisions in the brush.

State Bank and Trust Company in San Marcos, Texas.

94

Willis did not mention anyone else he used in the heist but there is speculation he had some help—possibly Herbert Holliday.

> *"The night we hit that San Marcos bank, a cold norther was blowing in. We looked around and couldn't find no night watchman so I went and cut the telephone wires right down the street.*

> *"Now the courthouse was right across from the bank and it had a big old yard planted in shrubbery. Once you squatted down in that shrubbery, why you could see down every street to see if anyone was coming. So I set Joe and Jess as my two guards out there to watch. I went in with Doc to work on the vault. It was a damn heavy drum door, it sure weren't no old cracker box door, so I poured in about six ounces of grease and blowed the door plumb through the window and over to the other side of the street on the sidewalk.*

Restored bank vault door that Willis Newton blew open with "grease" (nitroglycerine) in 1924.

"I thought there was just a square safe inside the vault, but found out that there was a round safe in there too. So I started in on the square safe and it took me about three shots before she come open. I got somewhere between $20,000 and $30,000 in money and Liberty bonds out of it. I never even tried the round safe and found out later it had $35,000 cash in it. What could I do, there was no way I was going to peel that blamed thing.

"They had a bunch of sacks of silver coins along the walls of the vault but we couldn't tote that to our hiding spot so I left it sitting there.

"About the time I was leaving the bank I seen two newspaper kids with stacks of the morning paper. I stopped and asked them, 'What you boys doing out this time of the morning?' They told me that they was working their newspapers.

"I told them, 'There's no use in selling those nickel papers. If you go in there and look, there's money lying all over the floor.

"Why just go on in and help yourself.' They just stood there looking at us as we cut across the courthouse shrubbery.

"When we got to where it was dark we turned back the other way and went down the rail road track two or three miles to a road crossing then turned and hit the highway.

"We went down the highway a bit to where we had our hiding spot. We laid there that night and our pickup man come out the next night and picked us up at nine o'clock.

"We jumped in and before you knowed it we was in San Antonio. We didn't have no hitches."

The next day after the robbery the newspapers were buzzing with reports of the "daring robbery." On January 6, The *Lubbock Morning Avalanche* reported:

Officers Believe Bank Robbery Carried out by Professionals

SAN ANTONIO, Texas. January 6—San Antonio officers who are working on the San Marcos bank robbery case are of the opinion that the robbery was carried out by professional yeggmen. The minute preparation with which the robbers performed their work led officers to reach this conclusion.

Telephone wires were cut, the town bell that is used to summon citizens on unusual occasions was put out of commission, a burglary alarm was disconnected and guards were placed on the outside to stop anyone who might try to interfere with the robbery.

The sound of the explosions awakened the whole town and vibrations were felt in nearby buildings.

Late Saturday officials of the State Bank and Trust Company, which was robbed at an early hour Saturday morning, estimated that $10,000 in cash and $10,000 in bonds had been taken from the vault, by the bandits. The bookkeeping offices of the bank were virtually ruined by the explosion.

Norman Jackson was a young man that worked in the grocery department of the store across the street from the San Marcos State Bank. He lived in an apartment above the store with his wife and baby. At about 1 a.m. that morning of the robbery, he was jarred awake by the explosion below.

He rolled out of bed and looked out his window to see the alarm missing from the bank wall. He threw on a pair of pants and raced down the stairs. He was intercepted by a man with a shotgun standing at the bottom of the stairs. "You had better go back inside sir," the man said politely.

Norman Jackson—witness to the San Marcos bank robbery.

Jackson lost no time in doing what he was told and shot back up to his room. "I had a double-barreled shotgun with two shells in it," Jackson recalled later, "but they were blowing the safe with nitroglycerin. I didn't want them throwing one of those little bottles into the apartment with my wife and my baby."

Another startled roomer, E.S. Sutton, made it out a back stairs and hit the street for the sheriff's office. All the while, Willis was repeating shots of nitro until he finally blew the door open. By that time all the windows had been blown out and money was floating down into the street. Jackson remembered that between each blast, the man setting the charges would walk calmly outside and then after the blast calmly stroll back into the bank.

After cleaning out the safe, Willis and the boys herded some gawkers into a bakery while Sutton Sheriff George Allen and deputy sheriff R.F. Magruder were stopped on an approaching street unable to get across some cut wires that were strewn over the street.

According to Jackson the whole episode took 45 minutes and then the gang (thought to have been as many as seven men) sashayed across the courthouse lawn and eventually trotted down the railroad tracks making a clean get away.

None of the Newton gang was ever arrested for the Sam Marcos robbery but the August 17, 1924 edition of the *San Antonio Express* ran an article that reported, "Investigations are being made by the Post Office Department of the operations of the Newton gang…has developed the fact that the State Bank and Trust Company of San Marcos, Texas, was robbed on the morning of January 5, 1924, by members of the gang." Apparently they never had enough evidence to pin the robbery on the Newtons though the article stated, "The agents claim that Willis Newton, Jess Newton, Joe Newton, Herbert S. Holiday and Carlos Fontano have been positively identified as men seen in San Marcos by several different people either before or on the night of the robbery."

The San Marcos bank building, recently used as a diner named the "Newton Gang's Getaway Saloon & Eatery."

Following the San Marcos job, Willis and his brothers lived the high life for a few months and then took a road trip to the Northwest where they hit a few banks outside of Spokane, Washington. They circled back through Montana and then ended up in Chicago during the spring of 1924. It was there that they worked their criminal contacts to set up the mail train robbery that would go down in the books as the all-time biggest score in American railroad history.

The Trains

"I can tell you it was a damn sight easier to rob a train than a bank. You was out in the country and it was dark. All you had to do was plan your getaway, watch the train, rob it and then scatter. It was a lot safer than robbing banks. They was hard work and dangerous."

It is difficult to pin point every one of the 80 bank robberies that Willis claimed he had pulled off during his career but the six train robberies are well documented. He pulled the first train job with a single friend but all the rest were accomplished with his brothers and others, notably Herbert Holliday and Brent (John) Glasscock.

Interspersing train robberies between bank jobs was Willis' trademark, hitting most of the trains of his career during the year 1921. As much as he heralded his heroic instructions not to hurt anyone during the heists, a black porter did die from gunshot wounds he suffered in the November 9, 1921 train robbery outside of Paxton, Illinois.

This is where historical research gets interesting. Hidden near the bottom of a front page of the *Carbondale Free Press* is a small article that blows a giant hole in Willis' insistence that he never killed anyone during in his robberies. The newspaper had covered the train robbery a few days earlier and reported that a black porter had been shot.

Cline, Texas

On December 29, 1914, Willis robbed his first train, at age 25. He had just been released from serving time in prison and met up with an old friend, Red Johnson. The two had gone to Uvalde and while there had broken into a hardware store to steal some Winchester 30-30s and ammunition for a pistol Willis was carrying. They decided to go to Cline, a small settlement west of Uvalde, by foot the day after Christmas with the intent of robbing the Southern Pacific Number 9 passenger train that passed through the station around midnight.

> *"Just after Christmas, me and Red Johnson set off for Cline (Texas) by foot. I knowed the Number 9 train came in there about midnight and took on water. So I told Red, 'Let's rob that train tonight.'*

> *"That night we went down to a little freight house near the depot. While we was waiting we took the linings out of our big overcoats to cover our heads and use as masks. When the train came in that night, we hit the back of it.*

> *"An old brakeman hollered at us and said, 'Hey! You can't get on here!'*

> *"I told him, 'Like hell we can't,' and I jabbed that pistol in his belly and he changed his tune. He didn't give us no trouble. We went in to the first car that was a special car for the superintendent of the Southern Pacific Railroad, old man Watkins. He was in there with another fellow. Watkins had a big old thick pocketbook and we thought we had a wad of money. Damned if his pocketbook wasn't full of them railroad passes and 40 measly dollars!*

> *"We went on up through the Pullman cars. We ain't never been in a Pullman car so we didn't know about them berths upstairs too. We just got the ones on the bottom and went through two of them. If we come up on a woman by herself we let her go.*

> *"When we come through the first car, we didn't know there was a drawing room in there with a rich old Mexican riding with his daughter. Sure enough, they had several thousand in cash and $15,000 in jewelry in a little bag up there. They was in a compartment car and we didn't know nothing about that so we passed them up.*

"Getting close to Spofford, we pulled the cord, stopped the train, and got off. In a few minutes we was hightailing it through them prickly pear flats headed toward Crystal City. In two days we were in Crystal City, sitting in my mother's kitchen.

"We got $4,700 off the train; more money than we had ever seen. I give Red half and we went down to the hotel and had us a big steak dinner. "

Along with the stories of ringing in the New Year, the Texas newspapers were ablaze with front page accounts of the "daring train robbery." The *San Antonio Express* quoted a number of first-hand accounts of the train robbery that vary from Willis' version, particularly in how they treated the passengers when they demanded their cash and valuables.

Two Bandits Awaken and Rob Passengers on Southern Pacific Obtain $7840 And Many Valuables; Overlook $16,000
Robbers Boarded a Train near Spofford And Escaped After 18 Minutes' Search of Passengers. Are Headed for Mexico
Posse in Pursuit Following Three Clues In Hope of Effecting A Capture Before Robbers Cross the Rio Grande—Mexican Who Saves His Fortune Reimburses Those Robbed.

...More than $7,840 and a number of watches, jewels, guns and other valuables were taken and $16,000 in gold was overlooked when masked men robbed the two rear sleepers of the Sunset Central Express train between Cline and Spofford about 2:30 o'clock yesterday morning. The robbery required eighteen minutes, during which time the bandits took the belongings of 14 passengers in the San Antonio sleeper at the rear of the train, and using W. F. Kendall, brakeman as a shield continued part way through another Pullman as the train neared Spofford, when the bandits retreated to the rear Pullman, pulled the bell cord and escaped.

Although posses organized by Ranger Phelps and

R. C. Watkins, division superintendent of the Sunset Central of this city, one of the victims, were organized at Spofford and Del Rio immediately after the robbery, no trace of the robbers has been found.

Two men discovered in a tool house on the Eagle Pass branch of the road were arrested and released. As the distance to the border is only about 30 miles by rail and about 33 miles by direct route, it is believed that the men are making an effort to reach the boundary line and cross into Mexico.

Jose Martinez, a wealthy mine owner of Durango, Mexico was overlooked by the bandits and remained the happy possessor of about $16,000 in cash and several hundred dollars' worth of jewelry. Martinez and his wife and daughter, occupied the drawing room in the front end of the last sleeper. They knew nothing of the presence of the bandits until aroused by the Negro porter, John Dunmore, who told him robbers were going through the train and that they had better hide their money and valuables.

The warning was heeded and the trio waited almost breathless for the appearance of the masked pair to search their compartment. Minutes that seemed like hours passed and finally Martinez returned to stick his head out into the car and learned that the bandits had completed their mission.

Whether due to their unfamiliarity of Pullman cars or to their haste, the drawing room was slighted in the holdup game, as were those occupying upper berths. Two men in the rear sleeper occupying upper berths were not disturbed by the bandits and one never knew anything about the occurrences until later aroused by the victims when inquiring about his loss.

He made an inventory and found his purse containing $200, his gold watch and other valuables had not been molested and were under his pillow where he had put them up on retiring.

Overjoyed with having escaped the robbers, Martinez summoned the porter who had warned him and his family of the danger and handed him a roll of bills as a reward.

Learning of the plight of some of the passengers who had been relieved of every cent they had and most of them of everything else of value, Martinez decided to share his good luck and wealth with his fellow travelers. To each he gave money in sums ranging from $25-$100 in proportion to their losses and other circumstances as he learned by personal investigations.

The newspaper article went on to detail how Willis and Red roughed up the passengers to get them to hand over their valuables. Contrary to Willis' self-described chivalry toward women, the article dispelled any doubts he was more than willing to accost women as well as men when it came to demanding all of their valuables.

...The bandits were described by passengers as brutes and were extremely rough at times in the handling of their victims. While several passengers were struck by the butts of guns in the hands of the robbers and more or less seriously wounded, not a shot was fired. At least four persons required medical attention after the bandits had taken their departure, and one woman whose name could not be learned, suffered an ugly gash in the head, which required 11 stitches to close. Exasperated at the thoughts of parting with her valuables, she first pleaded with the bandits without avail, and then she resisted their attempts to relieve her of her money and jewelry, when one of them drew his gun back and struck her across the head, inflicting an ugly gash and severe bruises.

One woman traveling with her four-month-old baby escaped brutal treatment and managed to save $185, which she had secreted under her bed. Occupying a lower birth in the rear car, she became hysterical when awakened and, looking out saw the masked bandits demanding money from the passengers. Time was valuable to the robbers and losing patience in their efforts to calm her, one of the men called out:

"Oh, let her go: she's nothing but a baby," and the pair moved to the next birth with orders to the brakeman to hurry and rouse the passengers.

One man who appeared slow in getting his money and time piece together was given a hard jab with the dangerous end of a gun and he dropped his money in this aisle of the car. Another rap from the gun and he was made to jump out of his birth and gather up the money and handed to the brakeman, who quickly passed it to the robbers.

One man who was a sound sleeper came within an ace of waking up in eternity when he failed to respond quickly to the shaking given him by the brakeman.

The robbers were not inclined to tarry and when the sleeper did not come across they were about to strike him a deadly blow, but the brakeman succeeded in rousing the sleeper and impressing upon him the seriousness of the situation just in time to save him from a beating.

One woman fainted and was quickly relieved of her money, jewelry, and purse containing her railroad ticket before she was revived.

This instance seems to awaken a strain of humor in the makeup of one of the holdup man, for he remarked, "If we could only put them all to sleep as easy—this would be the life."

Apparently some of the passengers were more than willing to exaggerate or totally fabricate their recollections of the robbery to reporters covering the holdup. In one case, a passenger identified himself as being the brother of the past president of Mexico.

...One of the first stories of the holdup obtained from an eyewitness came from Walter Grimmer, an employee of the electric light plant at Del Rio. Mr. Grimmer was a passenger out of San Antonio. He was riding in the day coach and declares emphatically that the two robbers boarded the train at San Antonio and sat almost directly across the aisle from him.

Mr. Grimmer says he was attracted to them almost as soon as the train left San Antonio by their suspicious actions and unusually tough appearance. He says a Ranger occupied a seat directly in front of him and that the men evidently recognize the officer and appeared to avoid his eyes whenever he looked in their direction.

According to Mr. Grimmer the two men waited until practically everyone in the day coach was asleep, when they left their seats and walked through the coach. Mr. Grimmer says he was awake at the time, watched the men walk through the day coach and saw them cross the platform and enter the first Pullman. He says he got a good look at the robbers and would easily be able to identify them. One he described as a man of exceptionally heavy build.

He says after going through the Pullmans the men signaled the train to stop and jumped to the ground on the moonlight side of the train. The aroused passengers saw them plainly as they ran. Both men are said to be Americans.

Benjamin Madero, brother of the late President of Mexico, is believed to have been one of the passengers in the upper berths who escaped attention. He arrived at the Sunset Station too late to get a lower birth and was consigned to the upper number five. Madero is supposed to have saved his belongings, although all of the others and excepting the passenger in the remaining upper, and the Martinez family in the drawing room, were robbed.

George Miller, a cattleman from Marathon was one of the passengers in a lower birth, and was robbed of his valuables. It is supposed that several hundred dollars were found in his possession.

Mr. and Mrs. L. T. Wood of 217 San Pedro Ave. lost their money and valuables when the brakeman awoke them and told them that the car was being robbed and to turn over everything they had.

Superintendent Watkins, who was asleep in a lower birth about the middle of the train, was one of the first to be robbed. He was relieved of $25 and pass books. Sam Scammahorn, a yard master at the Sunset Station, lost his revolver, watch and the pocketbook.

F. H. Bednarak, chief dispatcher lost his watch and some money. The three railroad men were on their way to a point on the Eagle Pass branch to hunt big game, but they joined the posse on the trail of the bandits.

C. D. Woodward, the Pullman car conductor in charge of the rear sleeper in the train, was not overlooked and the robbers relieved him of $156 including his own and the company's money.

Following this article that gave a vivid account of the pistol-whipping some of the passengers experienced during the hold-up, the *San Antonio Light* ran this front page reward notice on January 2.

$500 REWARD

The G. H. & S. A. Ry. Co. offers $500 reward for the arrest and conviction of the two men who robbed the passengers on train No. 9 on the night of Dec. 29, 1914 between Cline and Spofford, Texas, by order of Superintendent R. C. WATKINS

Apparently the reward offer worked; the January 21 edition of the same newspaper ran a bold front page headline.

Two Men Are Arrested As Train Bandits
Sheriff Johnson of Uvalde Is In San Antonio With Suspects.

The article went on to describe the arrest of two men who were working on a ranch near Uvalde. One was a recently released convict who had served time for burglary. Working on a tip, the Uvalde County sheriff sent two men to the ranch to surreptitiously identify the two men:

...Superintendent Watkins and W. C. Cox, both whom had been passengers on the train, went to Uvalde and, so as not to excite suspicion, went on a bird hunt to a ranch eighteen miles west of

Uvalde, where the two suspects were working. Both declared there could be no doubt as to one of the men and they believed they could identify the other as well.

As it turned out the reward was never paid to the informant; the case fell apart when one of the eye witnesses, a woman, could not positively identify the red-headed man. The law stayed on the case for a few more months and then slowly let it fade away. Willis was never arrested for the hold-up. For some reason he concentrated on bank jobs until 1921 when he and his gang reeled off three train heists during that year

Denison, Texas

After a long string of bank jobs, on August 24, 1921, Willis and his gang returned to train robberies. They held up the Katie Limited northbound on the Missouri, Kansas and Texas Railroad as it entered Denison early that morning. Initial reports said that the postal authorities were estimating that as much as $500,000 had been stolen. That estimate was later revised down to "less than $50,000."

Willis told the story this way:

> *"We had been watching trains coming into Denison from Dallas and we seen that there was a lot of registered mail bags being unloaded in Denison. I got John (Brent Glasscock) to come in and help us because you needed an extra guy to do the job right. I sent Jess to go to Glenwood and stay all night in our Studebaker. I told him were going to jump in that mail car when they pulled out of Bells.*

> *"In the summertime, when it's hot they left all the doors open on the mail cars. I told him that me and John would jump into the mail car and that we'd get that mail where the money was. We'd throw them mail sacks out when we was about two miles out of Denison.*

108

"Then we would walk back up the railroad tracks, gather the sacks and hide in the brush. I told Jess to come up the next night and pick us up.

"Well the train started out that night from Bells and I jumped in first with John right behind me. Son of a bitch wouldn't come on in, just stood there holding onto the door! A mail clerk tried to come out with his gun and I throwed my pistol on him and made him go down. There was another old boy trying to get his gun out but I'd throwed down on him too.

"And then there was John hanging onto the door, afraid to come in. Finally I hollered at him, "Get your ass in here!" He came on in, still just a shaking, but damned if he didn't start roughing up one of the men. I told him to cut that out, I did not want to hurt no one.

"So just outside of Denison we threw out the mail sacks and stopped the train. After we got them sacks we found out that we had missed the big money—there weren't more than a couple of thousand dollars. Hell, it shoulda been $40,000, money being shipped by the Dallas Federal Reserve Bank! Jess come and picked us up the next night but I can tell you it was slim pickings."

The *Denison Record-Chronicle* covered the story on August 25 with blaring headlines:

$500,000 Robbery At Denison
Two Masked Robbers Hold Up Katie Limited, Rifle
Postal Cars And Make Their Escape.
Two sacks of registered mail and several of
unregistered mail and packages taken by robbers
who overawed clerks.
Post Office Inspectors Working on Case without
Clue.

DENISON Texas—August 25.—Loot secured by two masked robbers who held up and robbed the Katie Limited northbound on the Missouri,

Kansas and Texas Railroad as it entered the city early this morning, may reach a half million dollars, postal authorities estimate.

Two packs of registered mail and several packs of unregistered mail and packages were taken.

B.J. Polk, postal clerk, who was hit on the head with the butt of a revolver when he failed to move fast enough for the robbers, was not badly injured, it was stated this morning. The robber apologized to the other mail clerks for his action.

No Estimate of Loot Given.

DENISON—August 25—Railroad officials after conferring with post office inspectors today declared it would be impossible to place an estimate on the amount of loot obtained by three bandits who held up the Katie Limited near here last night. Officials stated an estimate could not be offered before an official check of the registered mail was made. It was said, however, that there were no indications that there was any great sum of money obtained.

Asked concerning a report that $100,000 was taken from one of the sacks, railroad officials refused either to confirm or deny it. They declare that three or four sacks were opened and part of the contents of each taken. They pointed out, that the bandits evidently believed there was a big shipment of money on the train, but said they know nothing to indicate this.

Then in another article the newspaper reported:

News of Train Robbery Received Here over Wire Immediately after Holdup

News of the train robbery in the Denison yards, just outside the passenger station, was received here by the railroad wires early this morning almost as soon as it occurred. When train Number 1 on the Katie from Dallas to St. Louis was held up shortly after midnight by three masked men in the Denison yards, the mail cars entered, and considerable registered mail is supposed to have been taken.

The version referred here was to the mail car as the train pulled out of the station someone pulled the signal cord stopping the train. The mail clerks busy with their work were not aware of the intruders until told to, "Put your hands behind your back and stand fast." This was complied with and their hands and feet tied and they were laid on the floor of the car.

The robbers were said to have struck one clerk over the head with a pistol for not moving fast enough to suit them. The registered mail shipments were then rifled and then the mail sacks thrown off the train... The conductor put his head in the rear of the mail car and one of the bandits fired at him and warmed him to keep it inside.

It was said the affair was over in a few minutes and the thieves jumped from the car and disappeared into the darkness. It was not stated what the value of the mail taken amounted to.

In spite of Willis' account that they missed the big payroll and got away with a few thousand dollars, the *San Antonio Light* continued with the half-million dollar figure but included Willis' apology for Glasscock's pistol whipping of a mail clerk.

Mail Robbers Get $500,000 In Loot In Texas Hold Up
Sheriff and Posse At Denison Scour Country for Rifling Katie Train.

Denison, Texas. August 25—Sheriffs' posses today were scouring the surrounding country in a search for two masked, bandits who early this morning held up and robbed a mail coach in a Missouri, Kansas and Texas Limited train as it was entering the city. Although no complete check has been made, postal authorities estimated that the robbers' loot may reach $500,000.

...The bandits boarded the train at Bells, 13 miles south of here and after securely binding and gagging the mail clerks, proceeded to loot the car at their leisure. Just as the train was nearing the outskirts of Denison, it was brought to a halt by a pull on the signal cord and the robbers leaped from the car and disappeared into the darkness. They are believed to have been joined by three other men in an automobile, which was seen near the spot where the robbery occurred.

Before leaving the car, the robbers apologized to the mail clerks for striking one of their members, B.J., Polk over the head with a pistol when he failed to "move fast enough." Polk was not seriously injured.

Apparently this truly was one of the times Willis did not want to hurt anyone.

By August 26 the authorities were giving a different figure to the amount of loot stolen. The *San Antonio Light* ran this article as an update on previous accounts:

POSSES SEEK ROBBERS
Denison Superintendent Thinks Postal ' Robbery Amounts to $50,000.

Denison, Tex., Aug. 26.—Government employees cannot give an official estimate of the amount of money obtained by two masked bandits, who early Thursday robbed a mail car of the northbound limited of the Missouri, Kansas & Texas railroad near here. No trace of the robbers had been discovered Thursday night although sheriff's posses are searching the vicinity and a reward of $5,000 has been offered by Post office Department for the arrest of the men.

S. M. Gaines of Fort Worth, superintendent of the mail service for the eleventh district, expressed the opinion Thursday that, reports credited to postal employees that the amount obtained was approximated at $500,000 were exaggerated. While a thorough check had not been made,

Mr. Gaines believes that the loss will be found not to exceed $50,000.

The Denison area was alive with sheriffs' posses and within a short time they had arrested two men as suspects but had to let them go due to alibies. The last reported article about the robbery came on October

4, when the *Brownsville Herald* reported on two separate train robberies that occurred in Denison; the first on March 23 and a second on August 24 (the Newtons' job).

Denison Robbery Still a Mystery
Officers Follow Every Clue. But Obtain No Results, Amount Not Revealed.

DENISON, Texas October 4—Although federal and local officers have followed out every clue, one of which carried a postal inspector into Mexico, both of Denison's sensational mail robberies, the first of which occurred on March 23 and the second on August 24 remains mysteries. The amount of loot occurred in each case was never revealed although it was estimated that the thieves escaped with almost $200,000 in currency and bonds after the first hold up and that the second is said to have netted the bandits over $300,000.

On the night of March 23 while transporting a wagon of mail from a late night train to the post office. Two masked men stopped the wagon at the entrance of the alley just back of the federal building. At the point of a gun they forced the driver, a boy of 19, to drive to the Stevens School, in the North East section of the city. The boy was bound and gagged. There, the two masked robbers slit open the sacks of registered mail and divided the spoils.

After three hours the alarm was sounded. Several arrests were made but all were later released. One "tip" stated that the men were in Mexico, but nothing came of it.

The second robbery was staged on the night of August 24 as the Katie Limited was entering the city. Two masked men entered the mail car shortly after the train left Bells, 50 miles from Denison. After binding and gagging the three clerks, a systematic looting of the car was instigated. Several sacks of registered and unregistered mail were taken.

The engineer of the train saw a large touring car standing in the road near the spot where the train stopped and it is believed that the thieves escaped in this. Three men were seen near the car. Two suspects were arrested but established alibis.

So there you have it from the reports of the day; Willis and his boys got away with $500,000 or was it $300,000 or something "less than $50,000" when in reality they only came away with a few thousand dollars. Willis insisted most accounts of their robberies were overstated or "down-right lies." It appears he might have been right in this case.

Texarkana, Texas

At the same time they had been scouting the Denison train schedules they had also been casing the rail action in Texarkana, Texas. As a result, on September 6, they hit the Kansas City Southern passenger train Number 2 between Bloomberg, Texas and Texarkana.

"We knowed that a man come into Texarkana from Shreveport with a big express box once a week. He just carried it off the train and took it to the express office there in Texarkana.

"We got Joe to drive us to the little town below Texarkana where we had a place picked out where we knowed the train will be coming by sometime between nine and ten at night. Our plan was to get off the train there and walk to the hiding place in the woods and the next night Joe would come by and pick us up.

"So there was four of us, Jess, Doc and John (Brent Glasscock). I told Joe to take the car and pick us up the next night. At this little town called, Bloomburg, we jumped on the blinds of that express train. When we come to the Sulfur River, me and Jess went over the top and threw down on the engineer and fireman. I told them, 'Just when you get that mail car across the Sulfur River,

114

*you stop and leave all the rest of the train on the bridge.'
That was so nobody could get off the train because it was
on the bridge.*

*"The engineer did as I told him and as soon as he
stopped I ran over the top with a bottle of formaldehyde. I
threw the bottle down the air duct on the mail car. The
other guys hollered to the mail clerks to come out
because it was poison gas.*

*"Man, them boys throwed them doors open and got the
shit out of there in a hurry! The colored porter tried to
sneak out and get off the bridge but Doc threw down on
him and fired a shot near his feet. That porter made a
beeline back inside the train!*

*"We got the mail car uncoupled from the rest of the train
on the bridge but then we found out we had missed out on
the big express box. I grabbed one of the mail clerks and
asked him where the box was. He was stuttering and
stammering but he says, 'Mister, it didn't come tonight.
You can look all over but I swear he didn't come tonight.'
He was right; all I could find was a few registered mail
sacks.*

*So instead of several hundred thousand dollars we came
away with a few thousand in bonds and such.*

*"Well we went on up to the engine and got on. After the
engineer went and cut us from the rest of the train we
went on up to Texarkana and got off. I told engineer to
back the train all the way back to the bridge. Then there
wasn't anything else to do but walk back to our hiding
place in the woods.*

*"We laid out there in the woods until the next night when
Joe picked us up about eight o'clock. We drove to
Denison that night and two of us caught the passenger*

train to Tulsa while the other two drove the car to a
hiding spot and come on into Tulsa the next day."

Willis' account of the Texarkana train robbery is accurate but he
glossed over some of the major points reported in the Texas
newspapers. The *Galveston Daily News* gave a very different account of
the way they abused the engineer and the black porter:

Bandits Holdup Passenger Train; Mail Car Looted
Gas Bomb Compels Men to Open Door
Engineer and Negro Porter Injured in Resisting
Robbers.
No Estimate of Loss
Kansas City Southern, Train Is Stopped Just
Outside of Texarkana.

Texarkana, Texas. September 6—Four masked
men tonight held up the Kansas City Southern
passenger train Number 2 between Bloomberg,
Texas and Texarkana, looting the mail car of all
valuables.

Neither the express car nor the rest of the train
was molested. F. Woodson, engineer of
Shreveport, was knocked over the head with the
butt end of a gun, but his injuries were not
serious.

E. Moss, Negro porter, of Shreveport, was shot
in both legs. Postal authorities declined to make
any estimate of the loot, merely stating that
everything of value in the car was taken

The train left Shreveport at 6:56 PM being due in
Texarkana at 9:30 tonight.

About a mile north of Bloomberg, the bandits
entered the cab of the engine and commanded
the engineer to proceed to the bridge across the
Sulfur River where the stop was made with all
but the engine and the mail car on the bridge.

Two mail clerks in the car resisted the
commands of the bandits to open the car, where
upon a small gas bomb was thrown through the
transom, the gas compel the clerks to open the
door. Meanwhile, engineer Woodson had been

116

knocked out of commission and the porter shot.

...After the bandits left the car the engineer at their command went back to Sulfur River for the rest of the train, before coming in to report the robbery.

The two mail clerks, John B. Cheatam and Anthony N. Johns, the latter a negro guarding each side of the car, refusing to respond to the summons of the engineer who had been told to make them open the door, being threatened with death in the case of refusal.

The fumes of the gas however were so strong that the clerks were forced to submit to the bandits.

According to the statements of Cheatam, he claimed the bandits kept asking for "the big box," evidently believing that some shipment of value was among the contents of the car.

Disappointed, the bandits abused the clerks, jabbing them in their sides with their guns.

This account establishes a repeating pattern followed by Willis and his gang of not hesitating to abuse African-Americans when given the opportunity during a robbery.

The only person on the train to attempt to make an investigation was the Negro porter, who was shot twice in the right leg and once in the left leg, at the knees.

After the robbery had been reported the peace officers found tracks made by a large automobile at the point where the bandits left the mail car.

The four bandits all were young men; the clerks placing their ages at from 20 to 23 years, and all were light-haired. They wore overalls and jumpers, with handkerchiefs for masks and all wore caps similar to those usually worn by station employees.

Engineer Woodson, his head in bandages, two hours after the holdup took his train north to the end of his run at DeQueen, Ark.

The *San Antonio Light* gave details of the police investigation citing possible suspects and military training of the holdup men.

BANDITS USE GAS BOMB IN ROBBING MAIL CAR IN TEXAS
Texarkana Police Seek Four Men in Connection With Hold-up.

Texarkana, Tex., Sept. 7—Arrests are expected later this the day in connection with the hold-up of Kansas City Southern northbound train No. 2 last night, seven miles south of this city, the officers claiming to have information which they consider sufficient to warrant, arrest in the event, they can locate a quartette of well-known young men.

The four masked bandits are supposed to have boarded the train at Bloomburg, Tex., seven miles south of this city; they covered the engine crew, forced the disconnection of the mail car and compelled the engineer to pull this car to a point within two miles of the heart of the city, where the bandits left the train and escaped in a waiting automobile.

...Postal officials have not as yet given out information, as to the probable loot obtained in the robbery, though they admit the holdup men, secured everything of value in the car.

The use of a gas bomb with which to force the mail clerk to open the mail car leads to the belief one of the robbers was, an ex-service man, and had been in the chemical section of the army, officers said.

Obviously the police investigation proved to be off the mark, especially when it described two of them as, "well known to the police." At the time, none of the Newtons were well known in Texarkana and though Doc had served in the army, there is no indication that he "had been in the chemical section of the army."

Paxton, Illinois

Thirty days after the Texarkana job, the Newtons hit the Illinois Central passenger train outside of Paxton. Illinois. This particular train robbery is significant for two reasons; the killing of a black porter in the ensuing gunfight and the fact that it was over a year before the Newton's tried another train holdup. With so much shooting going on between the Newtons and the passengers on the train, it's no wonder they stuck to banks until taking on another train in November of 1921.

"Sometime in the fall we robbed a train south off Chicago where the line forks, one goes to St. Louis and the other goes the other way. We got on it at that junction. We went down there and drove the getaway car down into Indiana. We knew an old man from Oklahoma that lived down there close to Terre Haute, out on a farm. We could stay at his house and we wouldn't have to go into no town.

"At the junction, me and Jess caught the train. We had a bridge picked out to stop it on, and after about 20 miles we stopped it on this bridge. The rest of them was down there waiting for us. We took another fellow with us that sometimes we used because he was a pretty good driver. Joe and them was parked in a car out in a field about 300 yards away from where we stopped the train.

"We just told the engineer where to stop and leave all the cars except the mail car on the bridge, so that nobody can get off. We went back to get in the mail car, but the mail car man wouldn't open up. I knocked the windows out and still he wouldn't come out. So the engineer said, 'Let me in there and I'll bring out the mail.'

"But after he got in, the son of a bitch would not come out either! So I reached down to the axle box where the grease is and got me a big handful of that old packing stuff and set it to fire and threw it in the door. It wasn't a

119

little bit until it went to burning and smoking and they began the holler, 'I'm coming out.'

"I said, 'Just stay in there and don't come out this door or I'll shoot your head off' I made them stay in there until it was getting pretty close, and then I said, 'All right, come on out, and bring everything out with you.'

"All they brought out was just two or three small sacks of mail and the damned old mail clerk would not come out. When he finally did, I said something to him and he pushed me! I reared back and slapped him.

"By now the thing is just a burning. They got out of the train up there and somebody with a shotgun went to shooting. The old shotgun didn't bother me. We took them small sacks and went across to the car and this other guy with us had done run, the driver we had with us. Jess seen him running to the car and took after him. He got away and Jess said he was in the car when it started. Then the other three of us, we brought them two sacks, got in the car, and took out.

"We headed to Terre Haute, Indiana and on the way down there we opened up the mail sacks. We only got a few hundred dollars and a few thousand dollars in bonds. A puny piss-pot of money for the hell we went through!"

Willis' account fails to mention a large volume of details that appeared in the newspaper reports of the day. The *Carbondale Free Press* gave a detailed account of the train robbery; although, the newspaper's sentencing was confusing at times (text below is exactly how the paper reported the incident.)

Bomb and Rob I. C. Mail Train
Carbondale Mail Clerk on I.C. Mail Train with One
of Most Spectacular Robberies Present Generation
Object of Looters Was $100,000 Pouch of
Registered Mail, Which Was Supposed to Have

Been in the Car. Ed Reef and Two Other Mail Clerks on the Train. Battle between Bandits and Passengers. Clerks Beaten and Abused by Robbers. Soldiers Pursuit Bandits

Chicago, Illinois November 8—E. Germer, chief post office inspector, announced today the loot in the robbery of the Illinois Central train last night near Paxton would total about $400. They got two registered mail pouches and left two others. They overlooked a pouch containing $100,000.

Few robberies in the annals of outlaw history compare in the viciousness with a mail robbery four miles south of Paxton about 9:30 last night when seven masked men held up the Illinois Central passenger train No. 3. After failure to route the mail clerks out of the car, hurled through a bullet shattered door, incendiary bombs.

Flames from the bombs forced the clerks to leap from the car and turn contents of the car over to the looters. At the point of a gun one of the clerks was forced to enter the car of flames and bring out the registered mail pouch. The robbers then took the mail and escaped across country while the clerks and a few passengers witnessed the inside of the car eaten out by flames and reduced to ashes all but the steel hull of the coach.

During the robbery the robbers abused the clerks with revolvers by hitting them over the head, three more or less being seriously injured. Ed Reef, one of the clerks and a resident of this city, was the only clerk in the car who escaped the rough treatment at the hands of the outlaws.

J. Barrett of Mattoon was struck with a revolver and fell down a 12 foot embankment. Tom Baker, negro, was hit over the head, cutting the scalp severely and necessitating several stitches. Ben Bovinett also suffered a blow and a laceration of the scalp. The colored porter on the train was shot.

The masked men flagged the train and at the point of a gun forced the engineer to alight from his cab and go with them back to the mail coach. Compelling the engineer to accompany them back to the mail coach where they forced him to ask the clerks from the outside for a wrench to fix the engine.

At this request from the engineer Mr. Reef opened the car door and at that instant was covered with revolvers of three or more men. He slammed the door.

The holdup men opened fire through the door of the car and shattered the glass in the windows. This failed to either bring the clerks out or to force them to open the door. Through the opening broken in the door by the flying bullets, they hurled an incendiary bomb, which instantly burst into flames. The car filling rapidly with fire and smoke, the clerks then opened the door and alighted. Amidst the flames, one of the clerks was forced to enter the burning car and bring out the pouch containing the registered mail.

According to the newspaper account Willis and his gang's entanglement with the mail car crew drew the attention of the passengers in the rear cars, some who had firearms and came out shooting.

...Meantime, during the robbery, passengers in the rear coaches of the train, among them a number of soldiers alighted. The soldiers were anxious to shoot but the clerks were placed in front of the looters for protection. Persons in automobiles passing a highway near the train, heard the shooting and spread the alarm upon their arrival at Paxton. The Sheriff, a posse of citizens and officers rushed to the scene of the robbery in automobiles after the robbers had escaped.

The robbery was one of the most spectacular of the present generation. The train was stopped on a bridge, the mail card dynamited and set on fire and a continual barrage of shots between passengers and bandits was going on during the looting. No clue to the men had been found early today.

Some of the robbers boarded the train and made the engineer prisoner before reaching the bridge. There the advance guard was joined by other bandits who had come to the spot in an automobile. The engineer was forced out of his cab and used as a counter by the bandits to induce the mail clerks to open the mail car doors.

At this point passengers in the front end of the train began shooting at the bandits and the bandits usually replied with their revolvers while directing the mail clerks to throw out sacks of registered matter. The bandits searched the sacks in the presence of the victims and when they found no valuables made bonfires of the mail. Continuing the search through the sealed car, the bandits commanded the mail clerks to unlock the doors and threatened to kill the engineer and fireman who were then being held as prisoners.

When the mail clerks demurred some of the bandits placed a charge of dynamite against the door of the steel car and exploded it. The charge was too light and another was set. This was successful and mail clerks were ordered into the car to throw out packages. Thomas Baker of Carbondale, mail clerk, was among those injured he was beaten over the head with a revolver.

The account given by the *Edwardsville Intelligencer* gave a very detailed description of the people injured or shot during the robbery, particularly the name of the black porter.

Daring Holdup of Illinois Central Train Results in Mail Car Looting

Paxton, Illinois, November 8—One of the greatest manhunts ever held in Central Illinois is in progress today as the result of the daring holdup of an Illinois Central passenger train near here.

Seven masked bandits who participated in the robbery are being sought by posses numbering more than 500 deputy sheriffs, railroad detectives, and other volunteers.

...The robbers shot and slugged five men, dynamited the safe of the mail car and set fire to the car and escaped with several sacks of mail.

Arthur Moon, a porter who thrust his head out from his car to see what all the excitement was about, drew the fire of the bandits. He has two bullet wounds in his body and may die.

The others who were wounded are not seriously hurt. They include: Benjamin Bovinetti, Mattoon, Illinois, mail clerk, slugged and beaten; W. H. Bangs, Chicago, fireman, shot three times, but not seriously hurt; Thomas Barker, Carbondale, Illinois, mail clerk, slugged and beaten; J. H. Knowlton, Freeport, Illinois, passenger, slightly wounded by bullets; and an unidentified baggage man, bullet wounds.

...Two of the robbers were passengers on the train. As the train pulled out of here, they donned masks and climbed over the tender to the engineers. They drew guns and compelled Jack Fogarty, engineer, to stop the train.

As the train reached a bridge south of Paxton, the robbers forced the engineer to uncouple the engine and the express, mail car, and drive them a short distance down the track.

They then walked to the door of the mail car and commanded the clerks to open it.

The clerks opened the door of the car and saw the masked men with drawn revolvers. They slammed the door shut.

"Open that door or I'll blow your head off," one of the bandits yelled.

When the door was opened, the robbers compelled engineer Fogarty to enter the car and throw out the mail sacks.

Fogarty switched off the lights in the car but the bandits gathered a pile of waste from one of the mail bags, placed it on the floor, ignited it and by this weird light, sack after sacks of mail was tossed into the waiting arms of the bandits.

In the meantime Frank M. Williams, conductor

and several others of the train crew had crawled along the bridge from the detached passenger cars, and with drawn revolvers rushed toward the spot where the glare from the ignited mail car was lighting up the night. As the bandits saw them they opened fire.

Alarmed by the onslaught of trainmen and the spread of the fire in the mail car, the bandits withdrew after a few shots and sped away in an automobile that had been concealed behind bushes near the track

...Postal inspectors and railroad officials arriving shortly before noon on a special train at the scene of the daring holdup were amazed at the boldness of the robbers. They were unable to say how much the bandits obtained.

A.H. Germer, chief post office inspector of the Chicago district, scoffed at reports in circulation that the loss from fire and theft may reach an estimated total of $4 million.

"But it will take days to ascertain the actual loss," said Germer. "I can't say how high it will go."

This article is significant in that it names the black porter that was shot by the Newtons during the firefight with the crew and the passengers. A few days later a very small article by the Associated Press appeared on the front page of the *Carbondale Free Press*:

Colored Porter Shot in Robbery Dies Today.

Chicago. November 9.—The colored porter shot by the bandits who held up and robbed the Illinois Central train Number 3 near Paxton, Monday night, died in a hospital at Champaign today.

This confirms the death of Arthur Moon, the black porter who was hit by two of the Newtons' bullets. So, contrary to what Willis and Joe claimed many years later, they did kill someone in the commission of a robbery and this shatters their "Robin Hood" persona they tried to portray. Did they know about the man's death and chose to conveniently forget about him? It is hard to imagine that they missed the Associated Press release on November 9 when they usually took great pleasure in reading newspaper accounts of their robberies. Perhaps it was a simple error on their part but it does not seem likely.

A more sinister possibility lies in the fact that the gang had a propensity for treating black men with great brutality and the death of a black porter was not significant in their record keeping. A dead black man simply did not count. Though there is no evidence to support this indictment, it does follow a definite pattern.

St. Joseph, Missouri

Acting on a tip from "Des Moines Billy" that a $40,000 packing house payroll would arrive on a train at 11:00 that night, the Newton gang held up the mail clerk in the train yards of St. Joseph, Missouri. The date was December 8, 1922, a year after their last train job in Paxton, Illinois.

> "Sometime late in the fall of 1922 we got a tip that up at St. Joe, a packing house payroll would come in on the passenger train about 11 at night and it was unloaded on the side where it was all dark and one or two tracks over from the main depot. All the other trains come up on the other side, and they were closer to the depot. So, we figured it would be an easy take.

> "I told Joe to stay in the car with the engine running while we went into the yards. When the train came in there that night and they went to unloading the mail, throwing all them registered sacks off, why we hit them. Three registered sacks and we thought each one of them had money in it—payroll money. But damned if the money didn't come in the night before! All we got was a lot of bonds, Liberty bonds. The tip said there'd be $40,000 in there but we only got a couple thousand dollars in bonds.

"So we went on down to Kansas City and sold the Liberty bonds to a banker that give me $.90 on the dollar."

At this point in their train robbing career the Newtons seemed to be always just missing a good score due to misinformation or bad luck. The *Joplin Globe* still carried the paltry robbery on their front page.

Bandits Get One Registered Mail Pack in the Robbery
Clerk of C. B. & Q. Is Held up and Robbed in Union Yards at St. Joseph – Train in Route to Omaha.

St. Joseph, Missouri. December 8 (Friday).— Three masked men held up the mail clerk of Chicago, Burlington and Quincy train Number 23, in the Union yards shortly after 12:55 o'clock this morning and robbed him of one package of registered mail and five packages of first-class mail and escaped in a waiting automobile. No estimate of the value of the loot has yet been obtained.

The clerk had just left the train car and was carrying the pouches across the tracks at the station into the terminal, when he was intercepted by the men. The train was en route from Kansas City to Omaha. Two of the bandits carried revolvers and the third a shotgun.

When the train stops here usually three or four clerks go out to the mail car to receive the mail for St. Joseph, but this morning only one clerk went out to the train, but he was intercepted just as the clerk, R.V. Ott, from the mail car, was held up.

After obtaining the pouches, the bandits ran across the almost deserted station yard to a high-powered automobile waiting under glaring streetlights for them. The engine was running and as soon as the bandits stepped in the car, made off at a high rate of speed, turning a corner just a block away. That was the last seen of the bandits' car.

Capt. Kelly of the police department was notified at once and he now has all available officers and men scouring the eastern part of the city for traces of the bandits.

The Newton's train job on the night of December 8 was overshadowed by a much bigger heist in Kansas City. *The Moberly Evening Democrat* gave them second billing on a front page article.

Mail Bandits Pull Off Two Bold Robberies
Steal 84 Packages Worth $2500 at Kansas City and Rob Clerk in St. Joseph

Kansas City, Missouri. December 8—Bandits in two bold strokes were successful and robbing United States mail here and in St. Joseph during the night. A mail truck loaded with 84 parcel post packages valued at $2500 was stolen by the bandits here after the drivers were kidnapped.

Three masked men held up a mail clerk in the railroad yards at St. Joseph and escaped with a package of registered mail and two packages of first-class mail.

Kansas City authorities arrested four men early today in connection with the robbery here after the abandoned government mail truck had been found. None of the stolen packages were recovered. The robbery occurred early last night but was not discovered until Walter Holcomb and James G. Garner, freed themselves after being kidnapped and bound. They reported to police.

In the robbery at St. Joseph the mail clerk had just left Burlington train Number 23 when he discovered the bandits in the station yards. The robbers escaped in a motor car.

At this point it would seem that the Newtons should have thought that train jobs just did not pay off and that they should stick to robbing banks. That is exactly what they did—that is until June of 1924 when they went for the "really big score" outside of Chicago.

The Great Rondout Train Robbery

After the San Marcos bank job, Willis and his brothers went on a bank robbing foray through the Northwest. Then they returned to their old haunts in Chicago in the spring of 1924; they checked into the first class Strand and Blackstone hotels. While his brothers spent their days and nights enjoying the Chicago Cubs and the showgirls at the nightclubs, Willis was working his contacts for their next score. Eventually, he met with Jim Murray, a big-time crooked politician and beer runner.

James Murray—corrupt Chicago politician, beer runner, and mastermind of the Rondout train robbery.

Murray had inside information on all Chicago mail shipments coming in by trains, thanks to a high-living US postal inspector named

William J. Fahy. Preying on Fahy's penchant for wild women and betting on thoroughbred racehorses, Murray completely owned the inspector. Fahy could give the schedules and exact shipments of all registered mail coming and going out of Chicago—down to the estimated dollar amount of the mail cars.

On a regular basis, it was common for shipments of $1 million to $3 million to leave the Chicago station headed for the banks of the Northwest.

With Fahy's valuable inside intelligence and the execution of the robbery by an experienced gang, Murray told Willis "it was a lead-pipe cinch." Willis agreed and added that his men were not known to the local police; Chicago had always been their playground and they had never been arrested there. This was going to be the "big one" that would let the Newton brothers retire and live like kings down in Mexico.

The plans called for Willis to be the leader of actual robbery using his brothers, Brent Glasscock and Herbert Holliday. They would stop the train just outside of Rondout, Illinois, unload the registered mail shipment into two Cadillacs and drive about 100 miles to an isolated auto paint shop owned by Murray's uncle. They would split up the loot and then take off in different directions.

As an extra precaution, Willis had sent his wife to stay with her mother in Wisconsin so that she would not know anything about the robbery until it was over.

Train on the tracks near Rondout, Illinois circa—1924.

Willis told his story this way:

> *"First off, let me tell you Tulsa and Chicago are crooked towns; they are now and they always have been. It don't matter, crooks, cops, bankers or politicians—they're all crooked. It is just a matter of who is paying who and how much.*

> *"I knowed this guy named Murray in Chicago. He was a politician and big beer runner up there. Well, he had a crooked postal inspector on a string and he was planning on using his information to pull off some big mail train robberies. Murray sent a woman to find me and she come and told me if I wanted to meet the tipster (Murray's man) I could talk with him and find out the layout."*

Willis went to the meeting with Murray's man and was told they had information on all the mail trucks that carried money out of Chicago. The man asked Willis to go to the rail yards and see the truck deliveries. The two of them drove to the yards and saw six or seven trucks pull up to deliver the registered mail sacks. The plan was to hit the trucks before they transferred the sacks to the train. Willis was leery of the plan because there might be a lot of shooting and suggested they hit the train after all the trucks had unloaded and the train had pulled out of the station.

Murray's man said, "I don't know, that sounds risky."

> *"I went on back and said to my guys, "Let's find out anything we can about that train. This other fellow, he's a damned coward I'm not going to mention it to him anymore."*

> *"So we went to studying that train—where it went out, the best place to stop it was out in the country; where and how they loaded it at night, how it went out and if any law was watching when they loaded the train. We worked on that train for two months.*

"Then one day the coward comes to me and says, there is a $40,000 payroll going out to Cicero, Indiana every week. It gets out there real early in the morning and the post office only has one guy on that truck.

"That sounded good, so we went down there and looked over the layout. The tipster said, "There's three sacks of money going down there each week; a $40,000 payroll shipment."

"So on the morning of the job, I told the coward, 'Well, you ask the inspector to go and look through the windows.' He got back to us and said there was three canvas sacks of money set to go there in the morning.

"Well, we drove down there in a Cadillac, and when the truck came in, I was standing to one side and somebody was on the other side. One of our guys drove the Cadillac right up in front of the postal truck and we all threw down on him with guns.

"I sent Joe to the back of the truck with bolt cutters to cut away the locks off the back of it. Then someone hiked up into truck and throwed down those mail sacks.

"We got 10 sacks, piled them all in the Cadillac and took off. We went about 50 miles south of Chicago to some rough country where nobody lived. We had lined up a place to go to, an old shack way back in woods where we could layout during the day."

When Willis opened the mail sacks he found $35,000 in cash. After burying the sacks and mail locks they counted out a seven-way split of $5,000 each—giving Murray's man and the crooked inspector a share to divide between themselves.

"We was living with the swells on the south side of Chicago, staying at the Strand Hotel and the Blackstone

Hotel. Then Murray come to us with another job. He had an uncle who owned a paint shop in an old factory outside of Chicago and that was where we was going to come in with the mail sacks we got off the train. We was going to split up the money and layover until the next night.

"First, we stole two Cadillacs and planted them in a garage. They was high-class touring cars, one was a seven passenger and the other was a five passenger, both brand new 1924 models.

"By June the 12th we had everything in place so we met in a little joint in Chicago for the final planning. Joe, Doc and that piece of shit, John (Brent Glasscock) would take the cars down to where we would stop the train and unload the mail sacks. They left out early that morning for the road crossing that was about 2 miles outside of Rondout.

"Then me and Jess waited until it was dark and then we jumped onto the blinds behind the engine just before it pulled out of the station in Chicago. (Later, court testimony would reveal that it was Holliday rather than Jess who boarded the train with Willis.) *We had overalls and caps on to look like train men.*

"We planned it so me and Jess would go over the tender at Rondout and get the engineer and fireman to stop the train with the mail cars over the road crossing. Doc and the others would be waiting for us there.

"On this special mail train they ran it wide open most of the time and it was the second fastest train in the United States. The first mail car after the engine was where they carried the registered mail and that's where the money was."

As the speeding train neared the Buckley Crossing, the engineer pulled hard on the whistle cord to warn travelers that the train would be roaring through within seconds. Hearing the shrill blast of the train's whistle, Willis and his partner scrambled over the tender and confronted the two men in the cab.

"Jess grabbed ahold of the firemen and threw a pistol on him. I threw down on the engineer and he shot both hands up and began hollering to beat hell.

"I told him, 'I'm not going to hurt you. I want you to stop this train at that two mile crossing up there.' But he kept shaking and holding his hands straight up in the air and that train kept roaring down the track.

"I stuck my gun in my pocket and grabbed him by the arm. I told him, 'You better get them damn hands on the throttle and stop this train or I'll blow your head off!'

"The fireman was shaking too and he told Jess, 'Mister, don't point that gun right at me. I'm scared to death.'

"Jess says, 'By God brother, you ain't scared any worse than I am!'

"I finally got the engineer to stop the train but damn if he didn't stop it past the road crossing. I was mad as a hornet and hollered, 'Back this train back up and spot the first mail car right on that crossing.'

"He did like I told him and when we come to a stop I ordered everybody out of the cab. Then I told them, 'Now cut that car there. Cut the train right there behind that engine.' I didn't want nobody getting back in the cab and taking off.

"We planned for Doc to go over on the other side of the train from where we were going to unload the sacks and

watch for someone sneaking out of the train on that side. Joe and John (Glasscock) was on the unloading side and they was supposed to run down to back of the train looking for guards.

"When the train run past them that shit Glasscock crossed over to the side where Doc was and Joe threw down on the conductor and brakeman as they come out of the caboose. The brakeman gave him a story about needing to go back down the track to flag down any trains that was coming in behind us.

"Joe knew he was lying and that he would be running as fast as he could back to Rondout but figured it didn't matter because it would take him too much time to make it back there.

"After the brakeman cut the engine from the rest of the train, me and Jess took him and the engineer to the mail car. I couldn't see John and asked Joe about him. Joe said, 'Hell, he run up ahead somewhere. I don't know where he went.'

"That was just like the bastard to not follow orders but I didn't have time to chase after him so I hollered, 'Punch them windows out on that car,' and Joe smashed them out with his shotgun.

"I whispered, 'Joe, give me that formaldehyde bottle.' Then I hollered up to them guys, 'If you ain't coming out in half a second, I'm going to throw a bottle of poison gas in there and you'd wished you'd come out.' The door didn't budge so I threw the bottle through the hole in the window. Directly, they threw the door open and there stood 17 or 18 of them in there. I said, 'Just drop them pistols as you come out here.'"

Willis directed his men to collect all of the pistols and stash them in one of the Cadillacs. He then jumped up into the mail car and looking down on his prisoners, demanded to know the chief clerk. A man identified himself and Willis commanded him to climb back up inside the mail car.

He then told the man that he wanted all the registered mail sacks. Staring at Willis' pistol, the man quickly sorted through the hundreds of mail sacks stored in the car and pitched the sacks to the clerks standing outside. As the sacks were caught by mail clerks they were instructed to carry them to the waiting Cadillacs and stack them in the back seats and floorboards.

When they were loading the last of the 60 registered mail sacks, one of the clerks spoke to Willis.

"As we was loading, one of the clerks asks me, 'Is that your man that got shot out there?'

"I stopped and looked at him and said, 'There ain't nobody got shot out there.' The clerk come back with, 'Yes there was. I opened the door (to the other side of the mail car) and I seen somebody shoot a man.'

"Well, I damn well knew just Doc was supposed to be out there on that side. I run over to the door on the other side, leaned out and hollered, 'Doc!'

"Directly, I heard somebody moaning and muttering something. Doc had been shot and one of the bullets had clipped his tongue. So I went back to the others and I said, 'Go out there and get Doc he's shot on the other side!'

"Jess crawled under the train and damned if that shit, John, didn't shoot at him too! He missed and I hollered to him, 'John! Get your ass on over here!' When he came around to our side I asked him, 'John, did you shoot Doc?'

"The lying bastard swore, 'No, no, I shot a Hoosier. I shot a Hoosier.'

"I told him, 'The hell you did. You shot Doc,' and that was the last I said about it because we had to load up and get out of there."

The gang laid the badly wounded brother on top of the mail sacks in one of the Cadillacs while the mail clerks finished loading the last of the sacks in the other automobile. When they finished, Willis warned them to all lay flat on the ground until the cars had left.

It was nearing daylight when the two cars roared off into the darkness; Willis and Glasscock in the lead car with Joe, Jess, and Doc in the second car. After they had traveled about 30 miles Willis stopped the cars to check on Doc and pitch the stash of pistols into the brush.

Willis was furious with what he saw when he opened the back door to look at his brother. Everything in the back seat was covered with blood—Doc was moaning and writhing in pain from his wounds.

He returned to the lead car and controlling his anger ordered Glasscock to drive to their hideout at the paint shop.

They stopped to check on Doc one more time after they had driven about 50 miles. During that stop a mail sack fell out of the car that was later found by authorities the next day.

Finally, about an hour later, they roared into the open doors of the paint shop and then a short time later the mastermind of the heist arrived in his big touring car.

Not only did Glasscock's .45 blast a hole through Doc Newton's jaw but it also blew a major hole in Jim Murray's meticulous plans. When he arrived at his uncle's paint shop the place was in total chaos. A big pile of blood-stained mail bags littered the floor and Doc looked to be one gasp away from dying. The whole operation had gone terribly wrong.

The Newtons were threatening to kill Murray if he didn't get a doctor for Doc while Glasscock and Holliday were yelling that they wanted to cut the loot and get away.

Willis told it this way:

> "This Chicago guy, Jimmy Murray, pulled into the paint shop just after we got there. We told him what had happened to Doc and he told us not to worry because he could get a doctor.

> "He made a phone call and then he and Joe drove Doc over to a house that belonged to one of his hired men. They carried him up the back stairs in a chair and the woman that lived with the man opened the door.

> "Then a doctor come and worked on Doc and left."

A few hours later the first newspapers hit the streets with banner headlines blaring:

$2,000,000 Loot Taken From Train

Bandits Stage Sensational Holdup 32 Miles From Chicago; Use Gas Bombs to Subdue Guards.

Chicago, June 13.—In one of the biggest and most daring hold-ups in railroad history, four automobile loads of bandits last night held up a Chicago, Milwaukee and St. Paul mail and express train and escaped with loot valued at approximately $2,000,000.

Decatur Daily Review, (Decatur, Illinois)

The early reports that appeared in newspapers around the nation contained a wide variance of details and dollar amounts taken in the robbery. The *Bakersfield Morning Echo*, (Bakersfield, California) lead with the headlines:

Mail Train Bandits Get 1 Million
Postal Express Flyer Is Robbed North of Chicago
Three Cars Looted by Gang after Engine Is Detached

G.R. Williamson

Formaldehyde Thrown among Employees to Stupefy Them

Chicago, June 12.—A Chicago, Milwaukee and St. Paul mail train from Chicago in route to St. Paul was held up and robbed tonight about 11:30 o'clock at Rondout, Illinois, 32 miles North of Chicago by bandits riding in four automobiles.

A special train carrying express and government agents was commandeered here and sent in pursuit.

The bandits and train guards engaged in a pistol battle, according to the first information reaching this city and at least one of the robbers was reported shot.

The robbers took 40 pouches of registered mail containing bonds and currency from the Chicago Federal Reserve bank and consigned to banks in the northwest. Local bank officials estimated the loss at $1 million.

The train was due at St. Paul at 7:40 o'clock tomorrow morning. It was a solid mail and express train and carried no passengers.

The bandits set stop signals at the Buckley Road crossing, two miles north of Rondout.

As the train came to a stop two of the robbers boarded the engine and, covering the engineer and fireman, forced them to drive the train two miles down the line.

Before the train came to a stop two of the robbers boarded the engine and covered the engineer and fireman with revolvers.

In the meantime the three men who were on the tender uncoupled the locomotive. The robbers then forced the engineer to drive the locomotive to Rondout.

Three of the robbers rode the "blind luggage," or just back of the tender of the engine, according to Lawrence Benson, chief of the railroad special agents.

"As the train approached Rondout the robbers

pulled the air brakes, which brought the train to a stop," he said. "The robbers were strung along the tracks for the length of a car or two at almost the spot where the engine stopped," Benson said.

"Three or four of them forced the door in the first car. They were met with a rain of bullets from the mail clerks and guards in the car, but the robbers succeeded in overpowering them.

"One bandit however was shot. How badly, we don't know, although we found a pool of blood on the platform and there was a red trail from there to Buckley Road, where his fellows carried him and placed him in an automobile."

"The robbers then forced their way into the second car and then the third, but escaped unscathed from the rain of lead the guards and clerks fired at them and, as in the first car, they succeeded in overpowering the guards and the clerks.

The robbers did not go into any of the other cars, for they found 40 pouches of registered mail in the first three cars."

"Although there was a crew of 70 mail clerks and guards on the train of eight cars, they were all locked in and their instructions were that in no event were they to open the doors. They were all armed and instructed to shoot to kill anyone attempting to force entrance into their car.

The clerks and guards from the three cars were forced outside and lined up against the train. They were guarded by three of the bandits.

As soon as the robbers had gathered their loot they piled the sacks in four automobiles parked on Buckley Road.

The three bandits guarding the train crew made the crew turn away from the road as they retreated toward their cars."

None of the train crew was able to estimate the number of robbers. As soon as the word of the holdup reached Chicago all available express, federal and police officers were put aboard a special train, which set out for the scene of the robbery.

...The train carried 1500 mail pouches or about 50 tons of mail, local post office officials said. Of this there were 350 pouches of first-class mail, 40 pouches of registered mail, three carloads containing 350 pouches of parcel post and four carloads of American Railway Express shipments.

Buckley Road crossing—scene of the Rondout train robbery.

The *Decatur Daily Review* (Decatur, Illinois) provided an account by the engineer and fireman:

...The train had gone through Rondout and was traveling 60 miles an hour. Two armed men came from their hiding place and crawled into the engine. The muzzle of one weapon was pushed against the neck of engineer S. R. Waite, Milwaukee.

The other bandit covered the fireman, R. J. Biddle, also of Milwaukee. "A half-mile down the track you will see a red light flashing on the west side of the tracks," the man back of the engineer said. "When you see that light, you'll stop the train."

"If you don't you're gone."

The train roared on but with slackening speed as the bandits had ordered a slow application of the brakes.

At the Buckley Road crossing a red light flared close to the west rail. "Now jerk it," the bandits yelled into the engineer's ear.

Before the train came to a full stop, a third bandit cut the airline pipe. The bandits evidently were aware that only cars in the center of the train contained registered mail for the one covering the engineer directed that the train be slowly backed so that the middle car be stopped across the auto road.

This car contained the most important of the registered mail. Clerks in the middle car, sensing something was wrong, extinguished their lights.

The bandits ordered them to open the doors and when they refused the bandits hurled several bombs of gas through the windows.

This coach was in charge of Lewis Phillips, of Minneapolis, chief of all postal clerks on the train.

Someone from inside the car fired and was answered by another gas bomb. The clerks then opened a door and they were lined up beside the engineer and fireman, conductor and flagman. The latter two were caught by the bandits as they stepped down from the rear of the train.

The Davenport Democrat and Leader (Davenport, Iowa) reported that,

...The leader of the robbery put on a gas mask and forced one on Lewis Phillips of Minneapolis, chief of the clerks.

Before he had done this, however, he gave Phillips a course of instruction. "I want the Federal Reserve shipments," he announced. Phillips said he could not distinguish one pouch from the other.

"Well if you don't help me find the pouches I want, I'll kill you," the leader said. "I want the Federal Reserve shipments to Milwaukee, Minneapolis, St. Paul, Helena, Seattle and Spokane. I also want, for my own special purpose, a sack you have on board consigned to Roundup, Montana."

"Million-Dollar Holdup" Car

Mail car of the Chicago, Milwaukee & St. Paul railroad, held up by a band of more than 20 desperadoes near Rondout, Ill., and robbed of mail sacks containing almost $1,000,000 in money orders, etc. Arrow points to window through which tear bomb was thrown to overcome members of train crew.

Though fuzzy and of poor quality, this newspaper photo appeared a day after the robbery. It is still possible to make out the shattered mail car window through which Willis Newton pitched a bottle of formaldehyde to force the mail clerks to open the door.

The *Chicago Daily Tribune* covered the robbery with a dash of flair:

...The locomotive slowed to a halt in the lonely prairie country west of Rondout. As the pilot and his fireman dropped from the cab to learn why the signal had been given, a band of men swarmed out of the darkness and began shooting their firearms. Some carried sawed-off shotguns, others revolvers.

Half of them concentrated their attack upon the third mail coach. ...A fusillade of bullets and rocks crashed through the windows. The fusillade was followed by a tear bomb. The men rushed for the door and threw it open.

Meanwhile, another section of the bandit band had forced the postal messengers to open the coach ahead. They faced a battery of guns and a grim army of masked men.

"Get busy," the leader ordered. "Throw out those reds and chuck them in the automobiles."

A "red," in the parlance of the mail service, is a sack containing money. The crews of the two coaches were forced to fill the trunks of four machines with the registered pouches. Then they were ordered into their coaches and the bandits sped away. *[Willis swore there were only two Cadillacs used in the train holdup.]*

They carried with them one of their number who had been mistaken for a mail clerk during the heat of the battle and shot in the body.

...It was reported that the stolen pouches contained a heavy shipment of money consigned to the first Wisconsin National Bank in Milwaukee. There were also said to be shipments bound for Minneapolis, St. Paul, Portland and Seattle. The exact amount of the loss will not be known until today, when postal authorities check the registry slips.

An interesting historical side note to all the shooting that went on during the robbery was reported in the July 13, 2007edition of the *Sun-Times News Group*. It carried an article written by Larry Finley.

Wounded Rondout Schoolgirl Carried Train Robbery Bullet for Rest of Her Life
Girl was shot on way to school as historic heist of 1924 played out.

Rose Tomei carried a bullet embedded in her right side for most of her life. It was a reminder of the Rondout train robbery of 1924, which netted the Newton boys between $2.5 and $3 million.

The heist, believed to be the largest train robbery in US history, ended the careers of the four Newton brothers, from Uvalde, Texas, who were said to have robbed 80 banks and six trains from Texas to Canada between 1919 and 1924.

Ms. Tomei, a 9-year-old schoolgirl living in unincorporated Rondout, near Lake Bluff, came away from that day with a purple scar and a lump near her hip that pained her in later life, according to her sons. Mrs. Rose Emma Tomei, 91, died Sunday in Claridge Healthcare Center, in Lake Bluff....Her son, David, said the home was on a dirt street near the tracks where the Chicago, Milwaukee and St. Paul train robbery took place.

"She was walking to school under the railroad bridge near her house," he said. "She was nine years old. She was shot during that robbery. She just started running. She didn't know what was going on. She remembers all of the police being around there. The police told all the people to stay in their houses and stay out of the way."

"Her mother patched her up at home and the girl was examined later by a doctor," he said. "She showed the wound to me," her son said. "It was a dark purple area... on her right side just above the waist. They had doctors who went in people's houses back then and it was their opinion that if it didn't cause a problem, it did not have to come out."

Early on the morning of June 14, 1924, police raided the apartment of Walter McComb. Acting of a tip, they captured McComb and his wife, Jim Murray, Doc and Joe. The next day Willis showed up to check on Doc and the police arrested him.

Willis continues his version of the story:

"Sometime the next morning the law had worked all of their stool pigeons and come knocking on the door.

Jimmy Murray was there along with the guy who had the apartment and his wife, Doc and Joe. Joe was in the bedroom looking after Doc.

"Joe had told Murray to tell me when I called the next day, if he didn't answer the phone himself, for me not to come out there. But as it was Murray got himself arrested and he couldn't tell me nothing.

"I knew what apartment they was using so I went on out there and knocked on the door. They throwed that door open and shit fire, the place was crawling with policemen! I tried to put up a fight but it was no use there was just too damn many of them.

"Well, I sat there trying to figure a deal and so after a bunch of the law had left I come up with a plan. There was three of them and I told them I could give them $20,000 to turn me loose.

"They was all for it. So I called my wife in the morning, she was in Wisconsin and I told her to come on down to Chicago. My deal with the policeman was to hand them $20,000 when Louise arrived that evening on the train. Soon as they had the money they would turn me loose. I told them, 'I can get the money, but it will be tonight before you get it.' So they never took me in until later that day.

"Around five o'clock, just before we left for the depot to meet Louise, that dirty old rat Schoemaker, he showed up and damned if they didn't tell him the deal. They was all going to split the money and he said he was in on the deal.

"Lying bastard, he had planned to get the money and throw me in jail all along. This was his chance to make a big arrest and be a big shot!

"About six o'clock we went down to the depot and while we was driving down there I said, 'Now, I know a woman—I didn't tell them she was my wife—that's coming in that I can borrow $20,000 off.' So I met her with two of these lawmen that was with me when she got off the train. Schoemaker and the other guy held up at a distance away from us.

"When Louise come off the train I told her, 'I've got some friends in trouble and these are their lawyers. I want to know if I can get $20,000 off of you.'

"She said, 'Yes, I can get it out of the deposit box, but I have to go out to the bank.'"

The plain clothes policemen said they would take them to the bank and all four left in a cab. On the way, Willis kept his arrest secret and said nothing to his wife about the bribery plan.

"Old Schoemaker and that other guy hung back and watched us. When we got into a cab they followed us to the bank and waited outside. Soon as Louise come out with the money—it was twenty $1,000 bills—that dirty Schoemaker drives up.

"He piles out of his car and says, 'We're not turning him loose. We're going to take him to jail, and if you think of running him off, I'm taking you in instead.' He had just played along until he seen the money. I think he figured that it was some of the money from the train. But them idiots couldn't prove nothing with that money, because it wasn't mine. I had borrowed it off of my wife, and she didn't know that I was giving it as a bribe. So they took Louise one way and me the other. Finally, when I met up with her at the Chief of Police's office she said, 'What have you got him for?'

"When Schoemaker told her they had me for robbing a

train she looked him square in the face and told him, 'I know he didn't do that.' She was just as calm as could be.

"After we talked a little while they took me out to some podunk jail at Wheaton about 20 miles away and just left me there. She had to post a bond but they didn't file any charges against my wife."

Captain William Schoemaker of the Chicago Police Department.

According to the newspapers a few days later the police had arrested more than a dozen suspects, including the Newtons (under assumed names.) The *Murphysboro Daily Independent* reported on the arrest of those tending to Doc,

> ...Paul Wage, of Tulsa,*(really Joe Newton)* known
> as a police character, was arrested here today in
> connection with the hunt for the bandits who late

Thursday night held up and robbed the Chicago, Milwaukee and St. Paul mail train of currency and securities estimated at two million, five hundred thousand dollars.

Police announced they found a one thousand dollar bill and five hundred dollar bills on his person. The money, they said, "corresponded to a description of that the robbers secured. The bills were blood splattered. One of the robbers was seriously wounded by a fellow bandit mistaken for a mail guard. A man and woman giving the names of Mr. and Mrs. Walter McComb also were arrested."

In addition police took into custody a man giving the name of J. H. Wayne *(really Doc Newton)*, who had three bullet wounds; the prisoner said he was shot by a woman several days ago.

Another man giving the name of J. Mahoney *(really James Murray)* was arrested in a flat not far from where Wayne was taken.

All prisoners are being held ex-communicado *(really the word is incommunicado)*.

Then *The Billings Gazette* carried the arrest of others and the report that an airplane may have been part of the hold-up,

...Acting on a tip that the robbers would be found in a restaurant detectives late Friday raided the place and arrested a dozen men, including Dean O'Banion, Lewis Alterie and Earl Weiss, all alleged beer runners. O'Banion, Alterie and Weiss were seized a few weeks ago in a raid on a brewery here.

...In addition to the dozens seized in the raid, four other suspects were under arrest here and one man was being held at Waukegan, while posses of the deputy sheriffs and detectives continued to scour the country for miles around Chicago and patrol the roads leading to the city.

Confident that the holdup was the result of inside information obtained by someone connected with the post office or Federal Reserve banks, government agents at night were conducting a searching investigation of this angle.

A theory that the loot may have been cached by the bandits and then carried away in an airplane was held by some officials, Friday, after an airplane was seen to land about 2 miles from Rondout, Illinois, the scene of the robbery.

A checkup of local hangers revealed that no local planes were up Friday, postal inspectors said.

Mr. Germer said the scene of the Rondout robbery and the recent mail robberies at Harvey, Illinois, and Indiana Harbor had many similar features and added that postal authorities had been warned recently to be on the lookout for a band of Philadelphia criminals who were reported to be joining hands with Chicago robbers for a raid on the mails.

Dean O'Banion, beer runner and Chicago mobster.

With over a thousand federal, state and local lawmen rousting every known felon, things came into focus when they finally identified Jim Murray, the Fontano brothers (Ernest and Carlo) and the Newtons. Although they mixed up the aliases, The *Indianapolis Star* reported on June 19 that:

> Three brothers, besides the Fontano brothers, participated in the robbery, postal inspectors said.
>
> They are Willie Newton, Willis Newton and Joe Newton, alias Johnny Newton. All three are in custody. Willie Newton is the bandit who was wounded and who posed as J.H. Wayne, Willis Newton gave his name as Paul Wade and said he was a Tulsa, Oklahoma aviator, and Johnny Newton traveled under the alias of J.H. Watson.

Then a few days later *The Decatur Daily Review* gave a somewhat clearer picture of who had been arrested (without the aliases). It also reported that, contrary to what Willis said, an arrest warrant had been issued for his wife, Louise:

> Chicago, June 30—The arrest last night of Ernest Fontana, indicted with nine others on charges of participation in the $2 million registered mail robbery of a mail train near here June 12, narrowed the search today to Max Greenburg, the alleged "mastermind," Sam Grant *(really Brent Glasscock)* and Blackie Wilcox *(really Herbert Holliday)*, escaped from a Texas prison. Fontana was taken in a raid on a house in which he was concealed. He denied any connection with the robbery, saying he was home that night. His wife substantiated his story.
>
> Fontana is a brother of Carlo Fontana, who with Willis, Joe and William Newton, brothers, was captured Sunday. Also named in the indictments are James Murray, Chicago politician, Walter McComb, in whose flat several suspects were arrested and the three still at large.
>
> A federal warrant was issued last night for Louise Drafka who posed as the wife of Willis Newton and came from Milwaukee and obtained $36,000 *[Willis was adamant that it was*

$20,000] to buy his release. The action was taken to forestall habeas corpus proceedings for her release.

Murray also was served with a warrant charging him with mail robbery in connection with a million dollar holdup three years ago in Union Station. He was released on bonds.

Chief post office inspector R D Simmons said he would recommend that armed guards, probably Marines, be again assigned to travel with registered mail in the Chicago district. The indictments containing nine counts each were charges of robbery by violence and robbery with a dangerous weapon.

With Glascock, Holliday and Jess Newton on the run from the law, Willis continues with his version of the story:

"While I was out in the country they put Doc in the county hospital and slapped Joe in a Chicago jail. Joe said Old Captain Schoemaker told him he was going to whip the information out of him and he was going to put him away for 25 years in the penitentiary! He beat him straight for seven days!

"Glascock and the others had split up the money at the paint shop and took off before they could get caught. Jess took some money and come on back to Texas and John (Glascock) took Joe and my cut down to Tulsa where he hid it in his brother-in-law's house. Some of Murray's boys got his share.

"The cops then brought in the chief clerk off the train, and he identified me, Joe and Doc. I knowed we was dead fish because that bastard Glascock had run off and wouldn't help us. Jess had hid some of the money in a barn and then took off for Texas with $40,000 that Glascock had give him.

"So it was up to me to find a way to talk to Fahy, the post

office inspector. He was the main man but nobody in our gang knew who Fahy was but me. They never had no contact with him.

"*The city police had arrested me but then they turned me over to the post office authorities and sure enough Fahy was the head inspector among them. He made other inspectors talk to me because he knew I would rat him out.*

"*So I come up with a line to string them and I said, 'Yeah, the guys that was with us was Harry Wilcox (Holliday) and Sam Grant (Glasscock). Harry is a burglar from Texas and Sam Grant has escaped from the Walls where he was doing a life sentence for murder. I'm supposed to meet him in a saloon in St. Louis in a couple of nights. If you take me down there and let me go in and meet him, why you can get them both.'*

"*What I was figuring on was that if I got a chance to talk to Fahy I could get him to go along on the plan and let me get way in St. Louis. But I could never get to talk to Fahy alone.*

"*When they took me down to St. Lewis that bastard, Fahy, got the word to the newspapers that they was bringing one of the train robbers down to catch a fellow by the name of Greenberg, Sam Grant and Wilcox. Greenberg was a thief in New York City that I done business with sometime before.*

As it turned out the plan didn't work and I wound up back at Wheaton.

"*About that time Jim Murray had got out on bond. And then in a few weeks they come over to transfer me out of Wheaton and up to Rockford. It was Fahy and three more inspectors that come to get me.*

"All he had to do was get hold of Jimmy and he could've got a couple of guys to get the drop on them when they went in that jail to get me that night. It would have been simple for Fahy to do and I could have got away. But hell no, he wouldn't try to help me, not one bit.

"They took me out to Rockford and put me in the county jail there in a cell, up on the third floor by myself. I was in solitary—no newspapers, letters, couldn't see noboby; shit, they wouldn't even let me have a radio up there. I spent five months like that!"

While the rest of the Newton brothers were locked up in Chicago, Jess arrived in San Antonio with some of the loot. According to Willis, his brother hid the stolen money and then fled to Mexico.

"Jess had a few thousand stored away in Uvalde so he went down there, got it, and went over to Mexico.

"The law had tracked him down there and commenced sending men to drink with him, trying to see if the money he was spending was from the robbery.

"But it wasn't, it was some old money he had hidden way before we left for Chicago.

"Anyway when that didn't work they got him real drunk and told him, 'There's a bronc over in Del Rio that nobody can ride. We think you can ride him, Jess, and we're betting $500 on you. Will you go over tomorrow and ride him?'

'Why hell yes, I can ride him.' So the next day, Jess come over to ride this horse and they walked up to him, slapped handcuffs on him and said, 'We're post office inspectors and we want you.'

154

"They put him in jail in San Antonio but he got himself some lawyers. He and his lawyers fought for several months but he was finally extradited back to Chicago."

With Jess Newton it would be a real toss-up as to which he liked best—wild women, wild horses, or whiskey. As soon as he got back to Texas he went on a real bender in San Antonio.

Apparently, it took a load of whiskey to wash away the memory of seeing his brother lying on the garage floor gurgling on his own blood after the Rondout debacle.

During this binge, he took a taxi and headed out the Fredericksburg Road. A few miles out of town he stopped the driver, who was nearly as drunk as Jess, and took off into the brush. He hid his loot under a rock and staggered back to the cab.

A day later when he emerged from his alcoholic stupor and sobered up, he went back and tried to find the location of the cache. After several days of searching, he gave up and headed to Mexico. He then proceeded to continue his drunken spree by soaking up tequila in the cantinas of Acuna.

Federal agents tracked him down and pretending to be friendly tourists, bought him all the tequila shooters he wanted. When it came time for him to buy a round of drinks, there was another agent (sober) ready to buy the currency Jess used to pay the bar tab.

To their chagrin the bills did not match any from the Rondout robbery.

After many mornings of hangover headaches, due to too much tequila and the incessant mariachi music, the federal agents brought in Harrison Hamer to flush Jess back across the border into Texas.

Harrison, the brother of the famous Texas Ranger, Frank Hamer, was a Texas Ranger himself but at the time was working as a Mounted Customs Agent on the border.

All of Harrison's brothers were Texas Rangers and the family had a tradition of being lawmen. At six foot three, he was the epitome of the classic Texas Ranger and widely regarded as one of the best shots in Texas with either a rifle or a pistol. It was Harrison that came up with idea of baiting Jess with a challenge to ride a certain wild horse in the Del Rio rodeo.

Newspapers of the day erroneously reported that it was his brother, Frank Hamer that captured Jess Newton. This was later corrected by his grandson, Harrison Hamer (the 3rd).

In an obituary that appeared in the *Floresville Chronicle–Journal*, March 31, 2005. The obituary states that Harrison apprehended Jess Newton on July 4, 1924, at a rodeo in Del Rio.

> As he watched, he saw Jess come into the stands along with his wife and another woman. He waited until Jess got up to leave the stands and when he just passed near him he grabbed him by the arm and told him not to make a move and that he was under arrest.
>
> Jess told him that he "ain't going to do nothing." Harrison then took Jess down below the grandstands and asked one of the cowboys there to watch him.
>
> Harrison then went back and sent someone up in the grandstand to tell Jess' wife that Jess wanted her to come down for a moment, and as she passed by he also arrested her.

Texas Ranger Harrison Hamer, the lawman that enticed Jess Newton to return to Del Rio, Texas to ride a wild bronc in a rodeo.

Before they could get Jess back to Chicago, he hired a good lawyer and they fought extradition. Eventually, after exhausting all possible legal maneuvers, Jess was shipped by train back to Chicago.

At the same time the postal inspectors were trying to get Jess Newton back in Illinois, other inspectors were hard at work ferreting out one of their crack agents in Chicago—William (Bill) Fahy. Before Jim Murray had him firmly in his pocket, Fahy had a solid reputation as being a top agent among the US postal inspectors. He was credited with sending "Big Tim" Murphy and his alleged accomplices to the federal prison for the Dearborn Street station $338,000 robbery in 1921.

Murphy was a crooked labor leader in Chicago and Fahy had provided evidence that sent him to Leavenworth for four years.

"Big Tim" Murphy, Chicago labor leader and beer runner.

Willis credits the downfall of Fahy to a woman as he continues his story:

> "It was a woman that tripped up Fahy; a mighty fine looking Italian woman. I seen it happen to a lot of men.

> "They said that Fahy had arrested her husband for mail robbery a year before. She was damn good looker and after she got him drinking a lot she got him to talking— too much.

> "She thought she could swing a deal to get her old man out of prison and spilled the beans to the feds. Pretty soon they was watching him and arrested his ass!"

Acting on a number of tips and informants such as the woman Willis described, the postal inspectors laid a trap for Fahy and nailed him on August 27, 1924. The *Waterloo Evening Courier* described the details:

> ...Fahy's office and home telephones were tapped. Mysterious conversations were overheard between him and James Murray, politician and suspect released on bonds in connection with the case.

> Search of Fahy's files revealed that certain documentary evidence was missing. Investigators suspected Murray to be custodian of some of the stolen bonds, which could not easily be circulated because of their serial numbers being known.

> A trusted secret agent was to represent himself to Murray as a good man to push the sale of the bonds. But before the agent went to Murray, Chief Postal Inspector Germer told one man and only one of the plant. That man was Fahy.

> Fahy immediately was asked to attend a conference in a downtown hotel. All Monday afternoon and night federal inspectors conferred with Fahy.

> Late Tuesday, his eyes bloodshot and hands trembling, Fahy was escorted to his federal building desk where he slouched in his chair as US Deputy Marshals Howard and Carr placed him formerly under arrest.

> Fahy at first told investigators: "Yes, I tipped Murray off, but I did it in hopes of getting him myself. I tipped him off and told him he had better turn the bonds over to me. I wanted credit for the solution and recovery of the bonds. I was working as the 'lone wolf' as the boys call me."

> Coincidental with the alleged confession of Fahy, came the announcement that a delivery of $14,000 in bills, claimed to be a part of the Rondout loot, had been traced to the accused official. This money, according to a high federal official, was sent to Fahy by James Murphy,

recently arrested as a suspect in the Rondout robbery.

According to inspectors working on the case, it is believed Fahy is in possession of a considerable part of the loot, although they admit they have thus far been unable to recover any of that amount.

Rush D. Simmons, the lead United States Postal inspector that was successful in arresting the crooked inspector, William Fahy.

Next to be arrested was Herbert Holliday and then Brent Glasscock. Willis never mentioned Holliday but he was vehement about Glasscock, who nearly killed his brother, Doc.

"Like I said, Glasscock took off with most of the money. He buried a lot of it in fruit jars in that garage where we took the cars to. He gave Fahy $500,000 and then he took the rest to his brother-in-law's place in Tulsa.

"Then he took off for Michigan. Went to a damn health resort 'cause of his nerves and stomach ulcers! Some kid fingered him for a reward he seen in a post office. They got him and his two-bit wife."

On October 27, 1924, an Albion college student, Wayne Schaefer, was mailing a package at the post office in Battle Creek, Michigan. While he waited in line, he noticed a wanted poster showing a small blonde woman dressed in a nurse's uniform.

After staring at it for a second, he took the wanted poster off the wall and asked to see the postmaster.

He told the man that his dad had a rooming house in Battle Creek and when he was helping him with the storm windows at the boarding house a blonde woman came in and asked about a room for herself and her sick husband.

Within half an hour a postal inspector arrived and asked him to identify the woman from additional pictures.

"Yes, that's the woman. I haven't seen the man yet. I think he supposed to come by and pay for the room this morning."

Photographs of Brent Glasscock, using an alias, "C.P. Reese," and his wife, using an alias of "Ann Reese," were shown on a wanted poster that the boy had seen in the Battle Creek post office.

A copy of the wanted posters appears on the following page.

Case No. 65184-D   **Post Office Department**   Chicago Division
OFFICE OF INSPECTOR IN CHARGE
CHICAGO, ILLINOIS

$2,000 REWARD!

The Post Office Department of the United States will pay a reward not exceeding Two Thousand Dollars ($2,000.00) for the arrest and conviction of BRENT GLASSCOCK, alias C. P. Reese, who is wanted for his participation in the hold-up and robbery of Chicago, Milwaukee & St. Paul Train 57, near Rondout, Illinois, the night of June 12, 1924, in violation of Section 197, of the United States Penal Code.

SHOULD THIS OFFENDER BE KILLED WHILE RESISTING LAWFUL ARREST THE SAME REWARD MAY BE PAID AS THOUGH HE HAD BEEN TRIED AND CONVICTED.

Below are the latest pictures and descriptions available of Glasscock and his wife, Avis Glasscock:

(Taken in 1915)

(Taken in 1915)

(Taken in 1908)

Avis Reese.
(Signature of Woman)

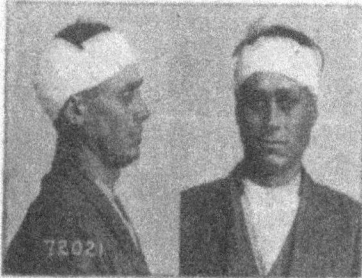

(Taken in 1917)

C. P. Reese
(Signature of Man)

The wanted poster for Brent Glasscock and his wife that was posted in all post offices in Illinois and the surrounding states.

Later that day Glasscock arrived and shuffled up the porch stairs. His wife was waiting for him on the porch and together they went in and paid the desk clerk for eight months' rent—in cash. After struggling up the stairs carrying a black suitcase, the couple was met by two postal inspectors who slapped on handcuffs and said, "Brent Glasscock, you're under arrest."

When the postal inspectors opened the black suitcase they found it contained $80,000 in cash.

The arrest of Glasscock was the lynchpin the federal agents needed to effectively prosecute all of the Rondout players. Up to this point they had recovered a sizeable amount of the train loot but they knew Glasscock could lead them to much of what was still outstanding. They went to work on him and within a short time he was confessing to everything, promising to tell where his loot was hidden, and most important of all, that he would identify Fahy as the "inside man" of the operation.

Picking up again with Willis' account:

"The feds really wanted to nail Fahy at the trial but none of Newtons had ever met him except me, I was the only one that did the meetings with Murray and Fahy. Not even Glasscock had seen him. The only time he ever seen him was when I pointed him out in the courtroom during the trial.

"The postal inspector running the show was a guy who grew up in Texas; his name was Aldridge.

"He knew Fahy had been the 'inside man' and wanted to take him down. The Italian woman got him started and after they watched him meet with Murray they had him."

Since none of the Newtons would testify against Fahy, Inspector Aldridge decided he had to get Glasscock to identify Fahy from the witness stand. After arresting Glasscock in Battle Creek, Michigan, the postal inspectors were ready to go to trial.

"After that Aldridge come and said if we would tell them where the money was he would work a deal where we wouldn't have to go to the pen for 25 years. He told me that the insurance boys wanted their money back and were willing to settle for short sentences for me and my brothers.

"About that same time another inspector told Glasscock that if he would testify against Fahy and Murray, he

wouldn't get no more than five years. Glasscock jumped at the deal and said he would finger Fahy at the trial as the 'main man' in the robbery.

'He also told them where he had hid the loot in the fruit jars and went down to Tulsa to get the money and bonds back from his hiding place in his brother-in-law's closet."

Brent Glasscock facing reporters during the Rondout robbery trial.

As the trial progressed, Glasscock managed to pull Willis aside and covertly ask which one of the men in the courtroom was Fahy. He had never seen the postal inspector during the planning of the train holdup. Willis told him that he was the one sitting next to James Murray.

"Then Glasscock got up on the witness stand and when they asked him to point out Fahy, he looked straight at him and said, 'That's him there, in the brown suit.'

"Hell's afire, I thought Fahy and Murray were going to have a conniption fit, sitting right there together in the courtroom. Glasscock was lying his head off but his testimony nailed it for Murray and Fahy. They was sent to Atlanta with a sentence of 25 years each."

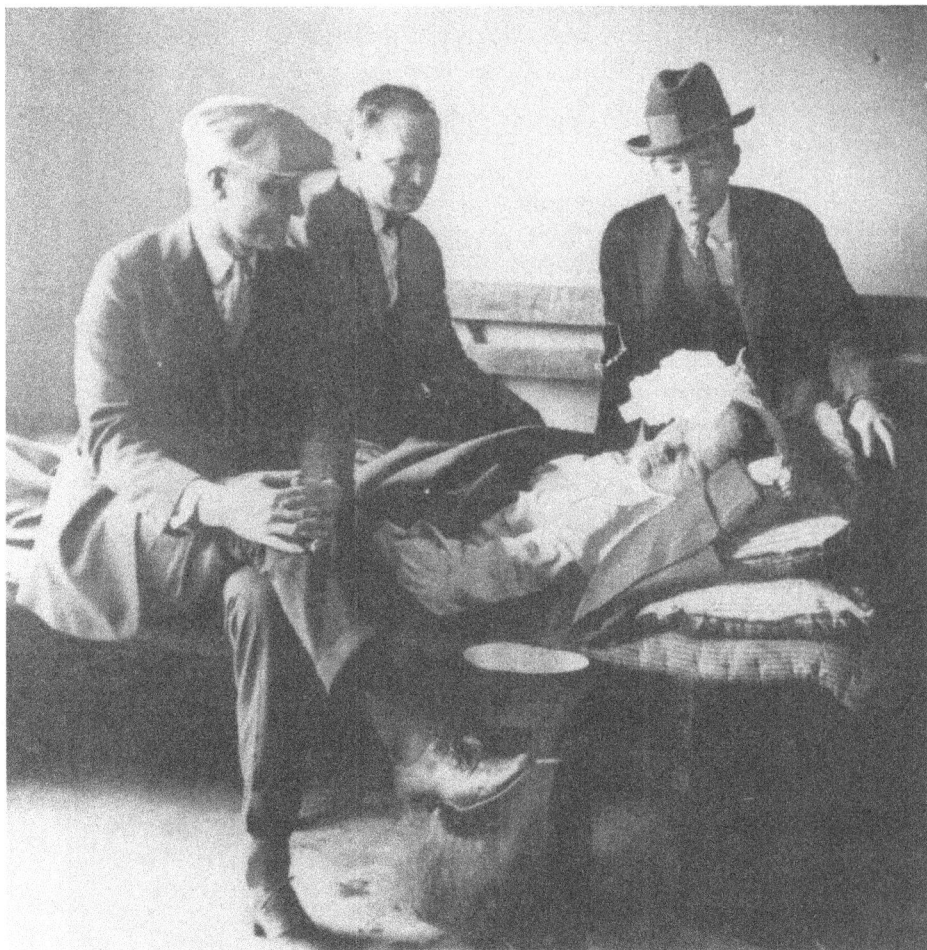

Willis, Jess, and Joe look after their wounded brother, Doc at the Rondout robbery trial in November 1924.

On Monday, November 8, 1924 United States District Court for Northern Illinois started the trial for the men accused in the Rondout robbery. Judge Adam C. Cliff was the presiding judge and there were 250 witnesses on standby to take the witness stand. After some preliminary remarks, Benedict Short, who was representing the Newton brothers, Herb Holliday and Brent Glasscock, asked to approach the bench. "Your Honor, my clients, Jess Newton, Joe Newton, Willis Newton, Wylie Newton, Herb Holliday, and Brent Glasscock wish to withdraw their pleas from not guilty to guilty, after advice from co-counsel." The judge allowed the change in their pleas.

So that left Fahy and Murray to face the jurors as the trial proceeded. On November 12, Jess Newton took the witness stand and his brother Joe followed. The *Wisconsin Rapids Daily Tribune* covered their story in detail:

> Chicago, November 18.—Plans for a million-dollar mail robbery in Chicago were first discussed in Kansas City, January 10, it was testified by Joe Newton, 22-year-old kid of the four Newton brothers who have pleaded guilty in connection with the $2 million mail train robbery at Rondout, Illinois, on June 12, last. Joe took the stand today and gave supplementary details to the story told by his brother, Jess, who with a broad brimmed hat in his hand and leather boots testified yesterday.
>
> Joe said James Murray, one of the conspirators on trial here, furnished the information. He understood Murray had information from a postal inspector. He said he and his three brothers met with Glasscock and Herbert Holliday, the latter of Kansas City, all of whom have pleaded guilty, on November 10.
>
> "Glasscock, said Murray, had a big mail job for us to pull off in Chicago, and he said some post office inspector had given Murray the dope. The job was worth 1 million, according to Glasscock," Joe testified.
>
> There was another meeting in Chicago a month later, the young Newton continued, and they were told Murray had seen the inspector in

question. The plan was to rob a mail train, he said, and that his brother Willie *(Willis)* investigated and said he was satisfied with what Murray told him about the inspector.

Fahy was named as having at one time, supplied inside information regarding a $100,000 currency shipment, and Murray is claimed to be a leader in planning the robbery and the subsequent hiding of the loot by Jess Newton, former Texas cowboy, one of the six accused men who confessed.

Newton, on the stand yesterday, told how his brother Willis and Herbert Holliday rode the blind baggage on a mail train out of Chicago and stopped it at Rondout where the remainder of the band waited in automobiles. After the robbery, in which Newton's brother, Willie, was shot by Brent Glasscock, one of the robbers, Murray sorted out the nonnegotiable loot.

Jess testified that he escaped and returned to Texas with $4,000, which he buried in four glass jars about 6 miles out of San Antonio on the Fredericksburg road.

When Newton and Murray finished their stories, Fahy, the one-time postal inspector, who has solved many a robbery, and Murray, were named for the first time. They were pictured as two of the three who did all the planning and bossing of the gang.

Brent Glasscock was named as the third, and he is expected to take the stand and finish revealing the inside of the plot today. He also has pled guilty.

Fahy was pictured by Newton as standing nearby while the gang waited for the holdup by mail truck on Jackson Boulevard—right in the loop he was quoted as giving tips on other planned jobs—but all the of them failed. Murray was named many times especially in plans to hide the loot.

Next on the witness stand was Brent Glasscock, who Willis said had never met Fahy and lied when he identified the postal inspector at the trial. The *Joplin Globe* covered his testimony.

> ...Glasscock took about two hours to tell all he knew of the robbery and then for a similar amount of time cleverly warding off all attempts of defense attorneys to tangle him up. He linked both Fahy and Murray directly with the robbery, detailing meetings between the three during which several other mail robbery plans were discussed.

> He pictured Murray as the actual leader with himself as the principal field marshal in charge of operations while Fahy gave information concerning movements of large sums of money and advised with the leaders of the holdup gang.

While on the witness stand, Glasscock admitted that he had served 16 months in a Missouri prison for burglary and 21 months in an Oklahoma prison for assault with intent to kill.

> On cross-examination...he said he would not consider holding up a train for only $100,000 but for 1 million or a million and a half he might take the proposition under advisement. This explanation was made in reply to a question as to why he did not try to stage a holdup after Fahy, according to his testimony, had told of a $100,000 payroll shipment going from Chicago to Georgetown, Illinois.

> Glasscock said that Murray and he had first considered holding up a mail truck here and had studied the movement of the trucks under Fahy's guidance.

In the same article Glasscock was confronted by attorneys about his shooting Doc Newton and his unsuccessful attempt to shoot Herbert Holliday. He was asked if he was trying to increase his share of the loot by eliminating some of the gang. He refused to answer on the grounds it might incriminate him.

The article also provided details on the recovery of some of the loot in Tulsa:

> ...How Brent Glasscock, alleged bandit who participated in the holdup of a mail train at

Rondout, Illinois, in June hid more than $1 million worth of loot in the home of his brother-in-law, Chester Van Cleve, Tulsa resident, without the knowledge of Mr. Van Cleve, is told in a news article the Tulsa World will publish tomorrow. The World credits the story to "authentic sources."

"It was learned here today that Glasscock, a former Tulsa gambler who was known here as 'Mizzou Number 2', came back to Tulsa about 10 days ago with five postal inspectors from Chicago, the World says, continuing: 'The party drove from the station to the Van Cleve home in a closed car. Van Cleve met them at the door and greeted Glasscock. 'Sorry to disturb you,' Glasscock is reported to have said. 'But there is a lot of money hidden in your house and we want it.'

"Van Cleve was astonished. 'Well, if there is any money here I don't know about it,' he told the officers. Guided by Glasscock, the postal inspectors went into a bedroom. The bandit leader climbed on a chair and then into a cubbyhole above a clothes closet. With his fingers he pulled loose a board and, shoving his hand in the hole, he pulled out a package of bonds and currency.

"According to his story he hid the money in the Van Cleve home without the knowledge of the home owner.

"Information that some of the mail robbery loot was hidden in the Van Cleve home was obtained by federal officers several weeks prior to the visit of Glasscock to Tulsa. A search of the house was made but the money was not found.

"The currency and bonds identified by Glasscock in court today consisted of $404,000 in bonds, $17,500 in currency and $7500 in unsigned bills.

"Van Cleve and Glasscock married sisters, according to records obtained by the World."

WILLIAM J. FAHY,
Accused Mail Bandit.

Newspaper picture of William Fahy.

On November 30, Murray and Fahy were found guilty and given 25 year sentences. Before Judge Cliffe pronounced Fahy's sentence he asked Fahy if he had anything to say. "Yes, your honor, I have been framed. My arrest record is good. I was instrumental in getting Big Tim Murphy convicted, who robbed the Dearborn Street station. No one believes me, but I swear to God that I am innocent."

Unmoved, the judge banged his gavel and gave him a sentence of 25 years in the United States Penitentiary in Atlanta, Georgia. At the sound of the gavel two US marshals rushed up on each side of Fahy and shackled him with belt chains and handcuffs. Without any further ceremony they ushered their prisoner through a side door.

Next Judge Cliffe turned his attention to the arrogant James Murray and asked him if he had anything to say before sentencing.

With a look of total contempt Murray stood up and said, "Yeah, I sure would. I hope you can survive Chicago, Judge. I'd hate to be in your shoes when Hymie (Earl J. Weiss) runs things."

The judge gave Murray a blistering rebuke for threatening him and then handed him 25 years in the US Prison at Atlanta, Georgia.

Earl J. Weiss, Chicago mobster.

Because they had pleaded guilty, a separate court hearing was held for the sentencing of the Newtons as well as Holliday and Glasscock. Willis described it this way:

> *"All of sudden that old Aldridge wanted to crawfish on what he promised me. He said he was going to recommend me and Doc get twelve years apiece, Joe for three years, and since Jess had cooperated so much he'd get a year.*

> *"Our lawyer told us, 'Hell no, you let these fellows up in front of that Judge and he'll give you every one of them 25 years. You let me go to Washington and I'll work a deal with attorney general and we'll get the sentences*

you was promised. He'll make a recommendation that you can give to the judge.'

"So that's what we done. We pleaded guilty and never went before a jury. Sure enough the judge took the recommendation and we got short times.

"They took us all to Leavenworth, Kansas. I did four years and two months, same as Glasscock. Joe served a year of his three years and then got out on parole for serving good time. Now Jess, because he was a good talker, got out in nine months. But hard luck always followed Doc; he had to stay locked up for more than six years because he had escaped from a prison in Texas before he joined up with us."

After the sentencing the Newtons along with Holliday and Glasscock climbed aboard a special train for their trip to Kansas. On December 12, 1924, *The Port Arthur News* carried the story.

> KANSAS CITY. December 12—Surrounded by a cordon of armed guards 14 prisoners, including the six confessed bandits who participated in the Rondout, Illinois mail train robbery last June, were transferred here today from a special car on a Chicago Kansas City train to a train, which will carry them to Leavenworth prison.
>
> Herbert Holliday and Brent Glasscock, two of the six were reticent and sullen. The Newton brothers—Joe, Jess, Willis and Willie—were in better spirits and chatted with their guards.

With reports that both Glasscock and Holliday had threatened to kill each other, it is easy to see why the newspaper reported their demeanor as "reticent and sullen" on the train to Leavenworth. At the same time it easy to see why the Newton brothers "were in better spirits and chatted with their guards" as a result of their light prison sentences

Even though by the end of 1924 all of the major players were behind bars, the story does not stop here. Though most of the

172

$3,000,000 loot had been recovered, there was still a significant amount that had not been found. Over the course of the next year there were a number of related arrests.

On April 11, 1925, *The Buffalo Sunday Express* reported on a major bust in Arkansas.

> Little Rock, Ark, April 11—Verner Heath, former tax assessor of Pulaski county was arrested here by post office inspectors last night on charges in connection with the hiding here last winter of approximately $100,000 of the loot of the Rondout mail robbery.
>
> Heath was the fourth man arrested here in connection with the hiding of the loot, which was said to have been part of the share of Herbert Holliday, now serving 25 years for his part in the robbery.
>
> Wallace Davis and Tom Poe, local attorneys, are scheduled to go on trial here on next Tuesday in U. S. court in connection with the case.
>
> At the same time it was revealed that J. C. McKinney, the other man arrested and who was indicted along with David and Poe is a government operative. McKinley had until today been thought to be a confidence man and was supposed to have been Holliday's cell mate in Chicago.
>
> McKinley, it was revealed, had been in the confidence of Holliday and other members of the gang that held up a Chicago. Milwaukee & Saint Paul railway train near Rondout, Ill.
>
> It was said that it was his work here that brought to light Holliday's share of the loot. McKinney carried out his part so well that no one suspected that he was other than what the post office inspectors had announced. At one time during his work McKinney escaped from government agents in Memphis. He was recaptured after a thrilling chase.
>
> The government operatives said today that all of the things charged against McKinney in the

working up of the case here would be charged against Heath who they allege committed the acts.

Further coverage of the Little Rock bust revealed a curious twist in the entire caper—the Newtons had apparently been filming themselves as they prepared for the Rondout robbery. *The Harrison Times*, on April 24, 1925, reported:

> ...Frank admission by Wallace Davis, former Atty. Gen. of Arkansas, and Tom Poe, young attorney, that they handled liberty bonds contained in the Herbert Holliday's share of the Rondout mail robbery loot, and confirmation of Davis's story of arrangements made for the return of $78,000 worth of bonds, by Major James Pitcock, Little Rock chief of detectives, were revealed in today's sessions in the trial of Davis and Poe.
>
> The two attorneys are charged in United States District Court with aiding in the secreting part of the loot in the robbery.
>
> A feature of the cross-examination of Major Pitcock by Assistant Attorney General Dyer was a series of questions about a motion picture film contained in Holliday's baggage. It was reportedly said to have showed Holliday and the four Newton brothers, all participants in the Rondout robbery, boarding an airplane in Kansas City and continuing on an airplane trip to Tulsa, Oklahoma, shortly before the date of the robbery.
>
> The film was at one time the subject of a search by post office inspectors. Maj. Pitcock testified it had been in his office and the inspectors could have had it if they had asked for it.
>
> ...Poe told in detail of his connection with the case. He denied ever having been told by Holliday or any other member of the family about the grip (suitcase) Holliday left in the Missouri Pacific station here, and which contained loot from the robbery. He also denied any connection with having the grip sent to Pine Bluff and obtaining it there, asserting that he never had

known of the grip until after his indictment. He is also denied having talked with JC McKinney about the liberty bonds.

Then in keeping with Willis' low opinion of the Chicago police and the rampant corruption permeating the entire police department, the *Joplin Globe* reported this little jewel on June 11, 1925:

Chicago Policemen Will Divide Bribe

Chicago, June 10.—The $20,000, which Willis Newton, one of the chiefs in the actual mail train robbery at Rondout, Illinois, last year, offered to the police as a bribe for his freedom, will be divided equally between four police officers, Superintendent of Police Collins said today.

Newton offered the bribe to the four officers in an effort to evade arrest. They accepted it, but he was held under arrest, nevertheless. They are Chief of Detectives William Schoemaker and Sergeants Fred Tapscott, Arthur Wachholz, and Thomas Griffin. Superintendent Collins said Corporation Counsel Busch had approved the legality of the division of the money among the four men.

Then on October 20, 1925, the *San Antonio Express* reported:

Officers Believe $400,000 Taken by Newton Gang Hidden Near Here

A confession, said to have been made by a San Antonio real estate operator, has started a new search for $400,000 loot taken by the famous Newton bandit gang in the Rondout, Illinois, mail robbery on June, 1924, and which is believed to be buried within eight miles of San Antonio on the Castroville Road.

The first clue in the confession is said to have been given in a casual conversation between Dewees and the man, who after many days of questioning and grilling has confessed to being a "fence" for the gang prior to and after the Rondout robbery, Dewees said. In return for his confession, the man has been given immunity from punishment.

The belief that the loot is hidden near San Antonio is further strengthened by the finding of the car in which Jess Newton and an unknown man rented in San Antonio four days after the robbery, Dewees said. In the car, located in a garage at Luling, were found several wrappers with which the stolen money was bound.

Securities valued at $1 million taken in the holdup, were taken to a place 16 miles from Chicago for division, according to the man's confession, and cash and unregistered liberty bonds aggregating approximately $400,000 were turned over to Newton and his gang.

After reaching San Antonio in considerably less time than the authorities thought possible by automobile, Newton and his unknown companion are said to have driven out on the Castroville Road with the "fence," his confession, said, where they were thought to have hidden the booty after sending the "fence" back to town.

Authorities are now attempting to locate the exact spot at which the loot is believed to have been buried, and which they believed to be within several acres of the point they have approximated. The new clues brought to light by Dewees show that the amount is many times larger than the $40,000 at first thought to have been the total.

During a period of six years at least five bank robberies in Southwest Texas were staged by the Newton Gang, the confession indicates in which more than $1 million was taken.

The whereabouts of the many automobiles used by the gang, which has mystified authorities, is believed to have been cleared up by the confession, which states the cars were run off a high bluff into Medina Lake when the bandits feared they would be traced through them.

New clues continued to be unearthed in the rapidly clearing mystery, Dewees said, and it is believed a solution of one of the most daring bandit gangs is near.

Strangely enough, with all that was supposedly revealed by the "fence" in this article, no additional charges were ever filed against Willis or his brothers.

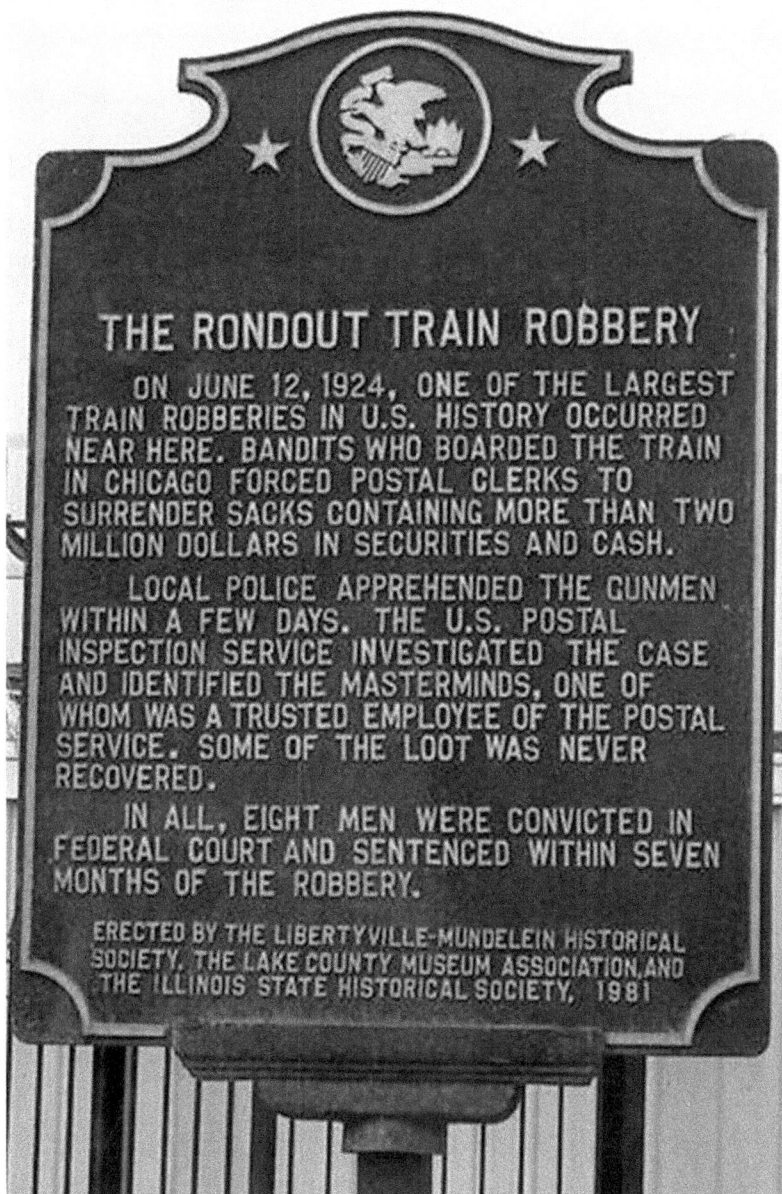

Historical marker in Rondout, Illinois detailing the 1924 robbery

Meanwhile upon his arrival at Leavenworth, Willis was satisfied that he had cut a good deal for the shorter sentences and thankful that they had all made it out alive—especially Doc. Now all he had to do was concentrate on doing his time and planning his next operation in Tulsa when he got out of prison.

Going straight was completely out of the question.

The Latter Years

Leavenworth

"Doing prison time didn't bother me none. I was doing one-third time, so they let me out the end of February, after serving four years and two months".

When Willis and his brothers arrived inside the walls of Leavenworth, they were greeted as celebrities. Among the elite of prison society were the mobster bosses and their henchmen but bank and train robbers came in a close second. The Newton Gang had pulled off a record breaking train robbery, got away with all of the loot, stood up to the beatings by the Chicago "bulls" and still managed to cut a sweet deal for light sentences. Every prisoner wanted to shake their hands and hear their story.

Leavenworth prison—federal prison where Willis Newton and his brothers served time for the Rondout train robbery.

After a few weeks the notoriety died down and the long days of monotonous prison routine set in for the Newtons. Willis described some of his time in prison:

> *"The first two and a half years weren't too bad. I worked in the tailor shop making them discharge suits they give you on your way out of prison. I had never done anything like that before, but in a week or two I was the head cutter. We did the best we could but them sack suits were plumb terrible looking—you could spot someone wearing one a mile off."*

Prisoners line up in a Leavenworth cell block.

The *San Antonio Express* on February 26, 1925, ran a small article on the Newtons' prison life, which contradicted Willis' assertion that he was working in the tailor shop. At the same time, the article repeated the often found confusion between Willis and Willie (Wylie):

Waukegan, Illinois, February 25. At least three members of the Newton gang, which participated in the $2 million mail robbery at Rondout, will be able to earn an honest living when they complete long terms at Leavenworth. Joe and Willie Newton and Brent Glasscock have been placed in the shoe shop; Jess Newton is washing dishes, while Willis Newton is in the hospital awaiting an operation. Willis was shot during the holdup. Sheriff Ahlstrom received a letter from Joe Newton Wednesday, in which it was explained what the gang was doing.

Later Willis did indeed have an operation after he was transferred to the steel working shop.

"My insides got to hurting bad while I was working in the steel shop. When I was a kid I had adhesions on account of the flu and I walked stooped over. Finally they went in and cut those adhesions apart. After I come to I was in a hell of a lot of pain but they wouldn't give me nothing. No morphine, no nothing, so I just lay there rolling ever which way.

"I was near dead when the head convict doctor, Bill Evans, come in and give me a shot of morphine. With all of my twisting and turning he told me I had torn loose some of the adhesions and I was humped up again.

"Finally T.B. White, the warden, come to see me in the hospital. He was from Texas and we talked about him being a Texas Ranger. In a few months he got me transferred to another room where they had a bunch of cots for people that couldn't work. I stayed there a year.

"Doing prison time didn't bother me none. I was doing one-third time, so they let out the end of February, after serving four years and two months."

On December 31 1925, Jess was released after having served his sentence of one year, deducting time for good behavior. At the same time Joe, who was sentenced to serve three years, was paroled.

Doc was the last to leave Leavenworth, having to serve out his full six years of sentencing. The first thing he did was to head to Tulsa, Oklahoma to join Willis in his latest illicit operation.

Newton Mug Shots

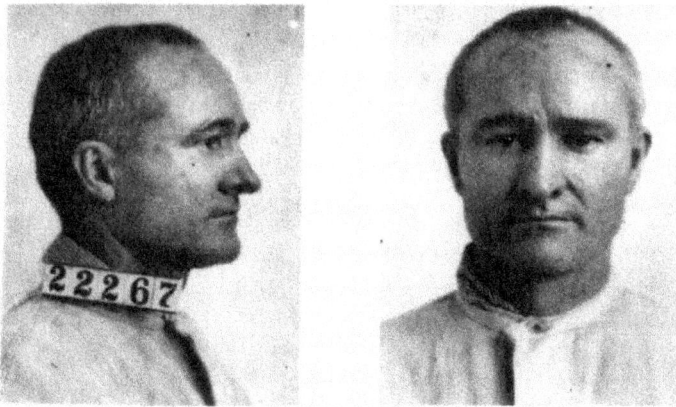

Willis Newton—Leavenworth mug shot.

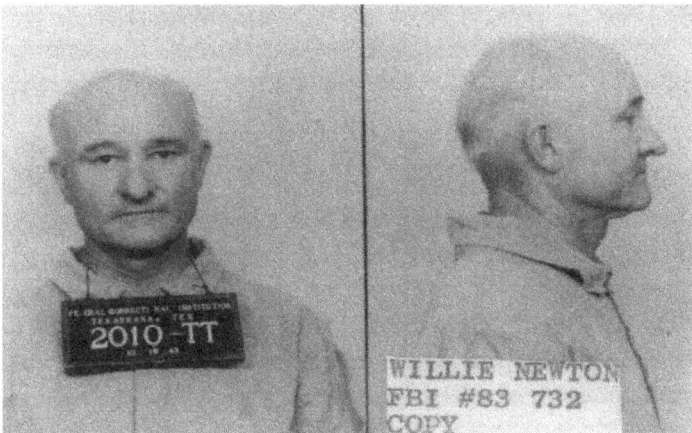

Willis Newton—FBI mug shot, misidentifying him as "Willie Newton."

Wylie (Doc) Newton

Jess Newton—Leavenworth mug shot.

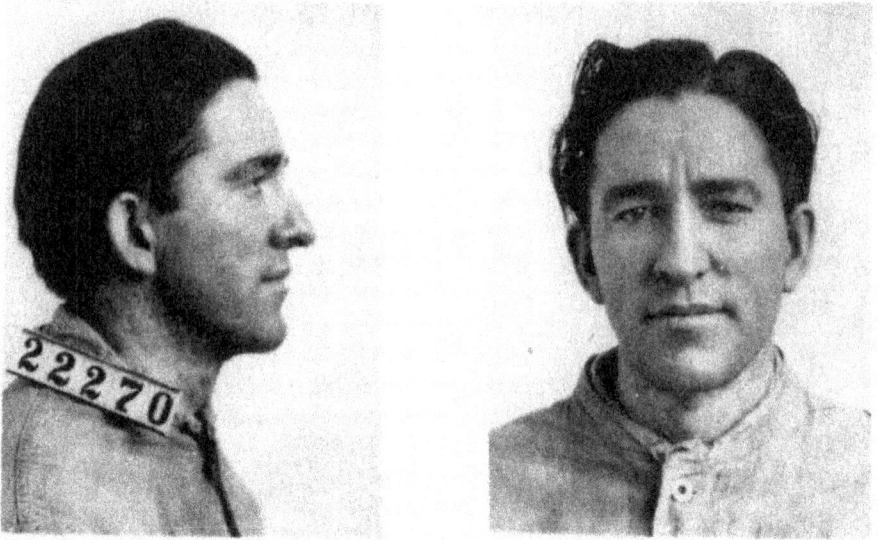

Joe Newton—Leavenworth mug shot.

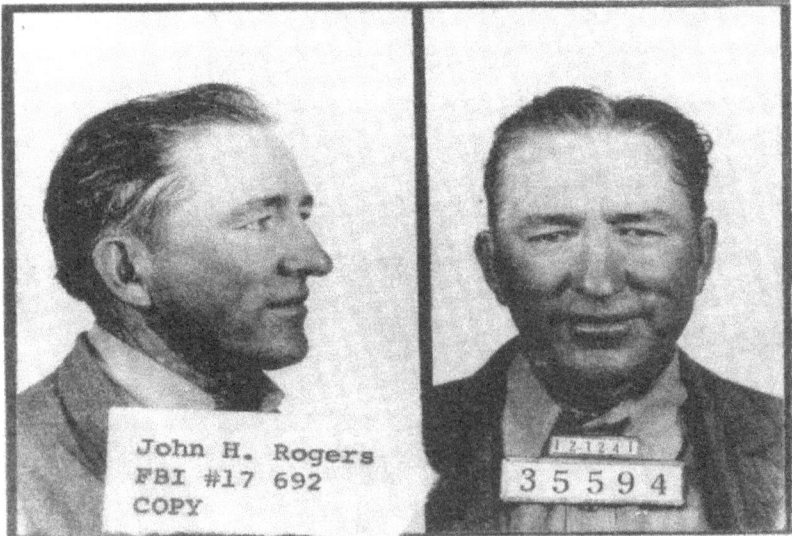

Joe Newton—FBI mug shot that identified him using his alias of "John H. Rogers."

Tulsa

"Like I said, Tulsa and Chicago was as crooked as they come. All the law was on the take. You could do anything you wanted as long as you paid the right people."

Willis' wife, Louise, was waiting for him when he walked out of Leavenworth. They immediately went to the Mayo Clinic for a thorough check up. After that they headed for Willis's favorite corrupt city, Tulsa.

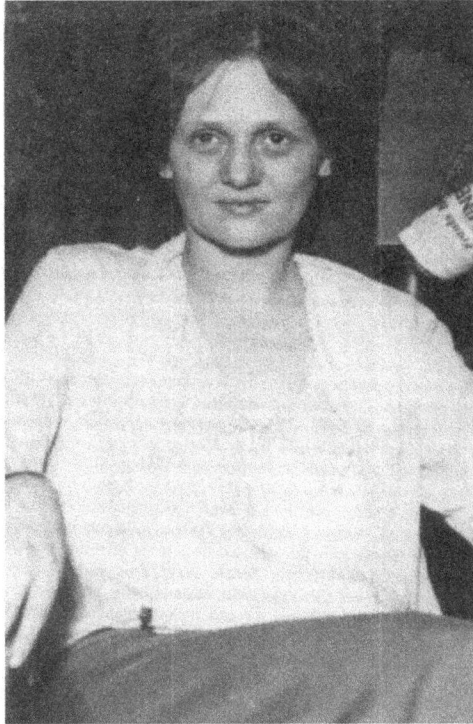

Louise Newton, Willis' wife.

Before the Rondout robbery Willis had bought some property in Chicago in Louise's name.

In less than two years the property had tripled in value and she sold it. This gave them $30,000 to buy a corner lot in Tulsa and set up a filling station.

"Like I said, Tulsa and Chicago was as crooked as they come. All the law was on the take. You could do anything you wanted as long as you paid the right people. I run this gas business for about three years and was making a killing because I was underselling all them big boys. Then a guy I knowed got out of prison and went to work for one of the big Texas gasoline companies. That turd-knocker went and told them I was the big train robber and I was out of prison on parole. Lying son-of-a bitch, I had a full pardon!

"So right away they went to the Tax Commission and said, 'You know what that ex-convict is going to do? He's not going to pay his taxes and close up. One day he'll be up and gone and you'll be holding the bag!'

"Well that done it for me, they wouldn't let me buy wholesale gas and I was out of the gas business. So I shut down my station and put in a drive-in café. I was selling beer and whiskey right and left. All I had to do was pay some of the law each month.

"There was this bootlegger over in St. Louis that had a big distillery that bottled whiskey to look like the real McCoy. He was my main liquor man and I was making a killing on the whiskey. Nobody knowed it was shine—they thought it was the high-dollar stuff.

"I had this guy I was paying $500 to haul a big load of the whiskey to me each month from St. Louis and I thought I could do it myself. The guy set the law on me and they arrested me for transporting bootleg whiskey. I couldn't fix the judge so I had to spend a year in prison.

"Soon as I got out, I built a big nightclub on my property and was back in business selling beer and whiskey. In a back room I ran craps tables and was making money hand over fist. Them soldiers [from the nearby military

camps] *come in droves, every night. Louise was at the door collecting a cover charge and she tended to all the money; put it all in a hiding spot at our house."*

Willis had his brothers working for him in the nightclub, though Jess and Doc spent most of their time drinking, fighting and generally carousing—sometimes firing off a pistol at some customer. Joe, on the other hand, was dependable. Joe was married and had a son, named Joseph Edward. Most of the family called the boy, "Little Joe."

With Louise managing the money, dressed in expensive clothes and furs, the nightclub managed to do a land office business—that is until a bank was robbed in a small rural town.

Medford, Oklahoma

"And the hell of it was they didn't have no evidence on us, none whatsoever! Everybody in Oklahoma knowed we didn't do it. Why, I had 50 business men from Tulsa vouch for me."

On the night of April 13, 1932, the First National Bank of Medford was robbed. Medford, located 135 miles west of Tulsa, is the county seat of Grant County and known for its low crime rate.

Shortly after midnight that changed when two men broke through a window and entered the bank. Then one of the men left the bank and entered a café a short distance from the bank. He held a handkerchief over his face with one hand and in the other hand he held a large revolver.

Ed Heiland was the night watchman, whose duty it was to guard the bank and other business during the night, was sitting at the counter drinking coffee and talking with the owner and another customer.

The intruder ordered those in the cafe to lie on the floor and stretch their hands out in front of them. He took Heiland's gun, then tied the hands of all three captives, and then forced them to march with him back to the bank. The prisoners were then put in the shadows near the bank building and held under guard.

Next, the man with the revolver went to the telephone exchange where he seized the town's night telephone operator (Edna Ciskowski) and forced her to make a series of calls to officers of the bank. After that the man severed all of the lines running from the telephone exchange.

As the various persons arrived at the bank, they were seized by the robbers, bound with ropes and herded into the lobby. As one man took charge of the captives, the second used an acetylene torch to burn through the four inch thick steel safe. It took him over three hours to get inside.

During this time, several other people came along. All were stopped by the man on the outside and made prisoners. This included two men driving bread delivery trucks and one man driving a milk truck. Before the safe was opened there were 20 people held as captives. One of them was a domino parlor employee, Willis Northcutt, who was commandeered to help the torch man by spraying a stream of water over the safe with a water hose.

The safe yielded $4,400 in cash and an undisclosed amount of bonds and traveler's checks.

In the meantime, Sheriff Ben Crider had been notified of the robbery in progress. He rushed to the scene but took up a position in a doorway, a half block from the bank. For fear of wounding some of the captives, the sheriff held his fire and followed the men in his car as the pair sped away after leaving the bank. He followed them west but lost them after about 10 miles.

On Sunday, November 20, 1932, Willis and Joe were pulled over in Chandler, Oklahoma. Inside their car the police found a double-barreled shotgun, three pistols, bullet proof vests, an acetylene outfit with tank, hose, torch, and goggles.

Initially, Joe had insisted that he was a welder and the equipment was used in his work. For some reason the authorities released him and turned him over to Texas lawmen who wanted him on a robbery charge at Decatur, Texas.

Willis was also released and he returned to Tulsa where he was arrested on November 27 and turned over to the Medford authorities. He pleaded not guilty but was ordered held without bond on a charge of robbery with firearms. Preliminary hearing was set for December 8.

In recalling the Medford robbery, Willis was adamant that he and Joe were innocent.

> *"Someone robbed a little old bank in Oklahoma and right away they blamed it on us. They robbed it with a torch and I never had seen a torch used on a safe in them days. And the hell of it was they didn't have no evidence on us, none whatsoever!*
>
> *"Everybody in Oklahoma knowed we didn't do it. Why, I had 50 business men from Tulsa vouch for me.*
>
> *"That old ex-sheriff knowed he didn't have enough evidence to convict me so he fixed the jury. He even bragged to a friend of mine after the trial was done that he had fixed the jury. Damn his hide!"*

During Willis' trial, the prosecution presented the Chandler police report itemizing the items they found in Joe' car. In addition, they had a number of the eyewitness accounts of the robbery from the people that were held captives.

None were more convincing than that of the telephone exchange operator. In a 1968 letter she (now Mrs. Edna M Mott) recalled her ordeal in Medford:

> *"...On a chilly night April 14, 1932 as I sat at my switchboard in the telephone office in Medford, Grant County, Oklahoma, I was taken by surprise by Willis Newton. He was cutting power lines and cables that led out of the office; it was about 1:00 AM.*

"A little later on, I, along with two other telephone employees, were walking down the street in front of Willis and his sawed-off shotgun while he barked his vicious warnings to us that he would shoot the first one that disobeyed his orders.

"He marched us down the street to Medford's First National Bank where his brother Joe was waiting with a few more Medford citizens they had tied up with wire and were sitting behind a tin grain bin, waiting for Willis to return.

"The bank was robbed; it had taken until a little after 5 AM to burn through the vault. One of the citizens was used to help accomplish the job.

"Believe me, I was one scared telephone operator. All I could think of was my four little children at home sound asleep in their beds and what might become of them if I was killed. I was their soul support.

"I called Willis a 'Gentleman Bank Robber' as he asked me if I was all right or cold. He put his overcoat around my shoulders and told me, 'Just do as I say and you'll be all right.'

"I shall never forget how big that gun looked or how black those eyes were that stared at me..."

The jury found Willis guilty and the judge sentenced him to 20 years in the prison at McAlester. Shortly after Willis' conviction, Joe hired a good lawyer in Texas and he was released on bail.

In a few months Joe, along with his wife and boy, skipped to Arizona.

McAlester Prison in Oklahoma.

Joe rented a house in Tucson under an assumed name and then quickly slipped across the border to work a gold mine claim he owned with some fellow Texans. From time to time he would return to Tucson for a brief visit with his family and then return to the mine, which was located near Sonora, 45 miles below the border.

According to his son, "Little Joe," on one of his visits, a man came to his house seeking money from Joe. They got into a fight and Joe threw him out of his house. The man tipped off the police and on Joe's next visit (May 23, 1934) he was arrested.

His arrest made splash headlines, but with a strange twist. The *Biloxi Daily Herald* reported the incident with a banner headline:

HOLD ROBLES CASE SUSPECT

Tucson. Ariz., May 23—An alleged participant in the nation's largest mail train robbery was questioned by authorities here today concerning the $15,000 kidnaping of June Robles, 6-year-old heiress. The suspect, Joe Newton, refused to make any statements regarding the kidnapping, in which the ransom was not paid, or the robbery of a Medford, Oklahoma, bank, the charge on which he was arrested here last night. Officers said Newton had been under surveillance for several days, during which time he had made nocturnal visits here from a mine in Sonora, Mexico, a locality in which an intensive search was conducted for the Robles girl before she was found. Sheriff's investigators said Newton made telephone calls to Tucson from the old Robles ranch between here and Sasabe at the border. They said they had learned he lived at the mine, with a brother, Tull.

Sheriff John Belton of Pima County said June had given him some information regarding the men who held her captive in a desert pit about 10 miles south of here and he indicated this information had led to putting Newton under surveillance.

June was kidnapped as she returned home from school here April 25 and found in the desert 19 days later by Pima county attorney Clarence Houston and her uncle, Carlos G. Robles, assistant county attorney.

They were directed to her hiding place by an anonymous letter from Chicago.

Joe Newton (above), was quizzed in Tucson, Ariz., concerning the kidnaping of six-year-old June Robles. An alleged participant in the $2,000,000 mail robbery at Rondout, Ill., in 1924, Newton was arrested on charges of robbing an Oklahoma bank. (Associated Press Photo)

This is a newspaper picture reporting Joe Newton's arrest in Tucson on May 23, 1934. He was questioned about the Robles kidnapping.

Apparently Joe did not have a part in the girl's kidnapping and he was summarily extradited to Oklahoma where he was tried for the Medford robbery and found guilty.

Willis described this way:

> *"I was working on appeals to my sentence when Joe was arrested and brought back to Oklahoma. When the jury convicted him they figured to give him five years but they left the sentencing up to the judge. That damn judge gave him 20, same as me!*
>
> *"While I was sitting in prison the governor sent word he'd let me out for $10,000. I said, 'Hell no!' Seven years later when a new governor come in he told me, 'Willis, you're getting a parole. I know you're innocent.' So the governor cut my time to fifteen years and said that after I served half of that, I was done. I got out a little after that but poor Joe had to serve a full 10 years."*

While Willis was doing his time in McAlester, it was left up to Louise to keep the nightclub running and manage the brothers, Jess and Doc. She held it together and bailed out the brothers when they were thrown in jail for disorderly conduct, basically drinking and fighting.

Willis took over the operation upon his release in late 1940 and stayed out of the headlines until he was plugged with a German Luger pistol by a hired killer in 1949.

Tulsa Shooting

Tulsa in the late 1940s was the scene of a major turf war between competing gambling outfits. Willis was in the thick of the fray, not giving in to any of the demands by the other gamblers. He knew he had to pay off the law but that was the end of it. With his background of using nitroglycerine he could play as rough as the others.

On September 22, 1949, the *Miami Daily Record* reported on a series of explosions at gambling houses with the headline:

TAVERN GUTTED IN NIGHT BLAST
Creek County Sheriff Also Probing Second
Explosion; Gamblers Suspected

TULSA, Sept. 22—A night club near the Oaks Country Club in adjacent Creek County was blasted to pieces by an early morning explosion today. An explosive charge placed about 100 yards from another nearby club known as the Blue Dahlia, detonated harmlessly with damage only to a few scrub oak tree.

Creek County Sheriff Lee Johnson said the blasts probably were the result of a gambling feud. Both establishments are on the Oaks Country Club road, south of U. S. Highway 66 near the Tulsa County line.

The destroyed club, a one-story concrete block and frame building, was one rebuilt on the site where another explosion nine months ago tore apart another building. Sometimes called the "Near Oaks Club," it had been padlocked by a Creek County court order for two months after officers reported finding gambling devices on the premises.

Creek County officials and the State Highway patrol said no one was injured in either blast this morning. Sheriff Johnson said no one was in the destroyed establishment.

Roy Farley, owner of the Blue Dahlia, said several persons were in his place but no one was hurt. J. E. Lowe, 47, an employee of the country club who lives near the two night spots, said the explosion at the Blue Dahlia came first. The second, he said, leveled the neighboring club and "nearly rolled me out of bed."

A quart of nitroglycerine detonated in your vicinity does tend to "nearly roll someone out of bed."

Willis was not taking any of the gamblers' guff, he was hitting back hard so it was just a matter of time until the other outfits decided it was time to hire a "hit man" to resolve their issue with this "country cracker." Sure enough, on October 1, the *Tucson Daily Citizen* ran a banner headline and this report.

Train Robber of 1924 Shot Mysteriously

Tulsa, Oklahoma. October 1.—Two gun Willis Newton, and one of four cowboy brothers who aided in a $2,050,000 mail train robbery at Rondout, Illinois, in 1924, was in critical condition today after being shot by a hidden sniper. The mysterious assailant fired two shots through a bathroom window last night at Newton's six room home in a middle-class neighborhood here. One bullet hit Newton under the right shoulder, pierced his lung and emerged near his left collarbone.

"Call the police, I've been shot," Newton yelled to his wife, who had retired.

Mrs. Newton said she heard a "scratching sound on the bedroom screen" just before the shot sounded. Outside the home, police found an empty cartridge from a German Luger pistol.

Detective Sgt. L N Hedgpath identified Newton as a member of the family, which conspired with several other criminals, including a postal inspector, to pull the 1924 robbery of the Milwaukee road's fastest mail train, No. 57, near Chicago. Hedgpath said he doubted that the shooting had anything to do with the old robbery, although $75,000 worth of loot in cash and bonds was never recovered.

He said it was more likely that Newton was shot as a result of a gambling feud here. Newton operated two nightclubs, the Shangri-La and the Stable, both of which were closed after recent gambling raids.

Newton lost consciousness shortly after the shooting, when he came to, he told officers he did not know who attempted to kill him but he "might figure it out later." His nephew, Joe, was in the house at the time of the shooting.

The nephew in the article was "Little Joe," the son of Willis's brother, Joe. Many years later, in an interview, he acknowledged that he was running a craps table for his uncle and was indeed in Willis' house the night of the shooting.

Contrary to the news reports, the bullet lodged in Willis' back, near the spine. The doctors decided it would be dangerous to try and remove the slug and he would carry it with him the rest of his life.

After he recovered from the shooting, Willis and Louise wrapped up their businesses in Tulsa and headed back to Uvalde, Texas, ostensibly to "retire to a quiet, law abiding life."

Well, not exactly.

During his Tulsa days Willis had operated a number of night clubs—the Music Box, the Shangri-La, the Stable, and the Buckhorn Palace. A short time after arriving in Texas, he bought some land on Mustang Island. At the time, the island could only be reached by a ferry that ran from Aransas Pass to Port Aransas. Perfect for his next joint, named the Buckhorn Palace (he liked that name).

Willis spent a large sum of money over the next year building the night club, designed to offer booze and craps shooting. He paid ferry operators to call him when they brought lawmen over to the island so that all evidence of illegal activity would be hidden by the time they arrived. It was a well-planned operation and within a short time he was doing a brisk business—too brisk. The other illegal operators did not like the competition.

One night, while the Buckhorn Palace was closed, a fire bomb was hurled through the front of building. "Little Joe," who was asleep on the second floor, heard the blast and saw the smoke coming in under his door. With no other choice, he jumped out a side window and injured his left ankle. Hobbling off into the darkness he was able to elude the men with guns who came looking for him. Later, when the police arrived, he appeared and told them what had happened. Willis arrived the next day, surveyed the charred remains of his joint and took Joe to a doctor.

With fire-bombing of the Buckhorn Palace, Willis decided his days of fighting other outfits was over and sold the Mustang Island property. Then over the next decade he managed to keep a very low profile living with his wife in Uvalde.

Louise Newton, known as "Mammy" by the family and close friends, died of heart trouble on December 22, 1959. The loss of his wife was more than an emotional loss; it was a financial disaster for Willis. She had always managed their money and curbed Willis' penchant for blowing their money.

Shortly before Louise's death, Willis had "acquired" a large diamond that he was planning to have set in a ring for his wife. With her gone he knew he would eventually have to sell the diamond and other jewelry to survive. That is where Frank Brent, his nephew, comes into the story.

⸺⸺•••●●●●••⸺⸺•

G.R. Williamson

Frank Brent & the Big Diamond

"I was taking a statement from him—every time he quit talking I'd tighten that chain a little tighter."

Over the next few years Willis had various members of his family move in with him for short stays, mainly to tap him for money. In 1962, his nephew Frank Brent drifted in for a few months and then abruptly loaded up his things and headed for Tulsa. A week later, Willis noticed the "big diamond" and some other jewelry was missing. He contacted a local lawman, Kenneth Kelley, to investigate the missing items.

In a later interview, Mr. Kelley, a popular and highly respected sheriff of Uvalde County, chuckled as he recalled the incident:

"I had known Willis for several years and even though I had to arrest him a few times (for minor offences) we got along fairly well. Well one morning, I get this call from Willis. He wants me to come over to his house to investigate a missing big diamond. I went over there and he showed me where the jewelry was normally kept. Sure enough nothing was there. I asked him where Frank was and he said that he had left the previous week.

"I told him, 'Well there you go. Frank took it with him.'

"Willis shook his head. 'Naw, it couldn't have been him, I treated him like he was my son.'

"I looked him square in the face and said, 'Willis, think about it. Frank's gone and so is the diamond. It's as simple as that.'

"I left and then the next day I get a call from Willis wanting me to go with him up to Tulsa. He wanted me to go with him and find Frank. When I said no he said he would hire me and pay double what I was getting. I told

199

him there was no way in hell I was going to do that and suggested he get someone in his family to drive him up there to Tulsa.

"Willis did exactly that, he went up there with his nephew from Corpus Christi. They kidnapped Frank, had him in the back of Willis' car, chained to a engine block. They was just out of town, near the lake, when a woman come along and saw them. The driver had a bandanna tied around his face and Willis was in the back with a gun. She called the police and they went out and caught them.

"They kept them out there in Tulsa for about three months and finally when Willis got back he said, 'All they wanted was to build them an elevator in their jail. I paid $30,000 for that and they turned me loose.'

"Knowing Willis I just had to ask him, 'what was you doing with Frank chained down in your back seat?'

"I was taking a statement from him—every time he quit talking I'd tighten that chain a little tighter.'

"It was all I could do to keep from laughing but I asked him what he was going to do with him when he got through taking his statement.

"I was going to see if he could swim that Tulsa lake with that engine block chained to his neck.'

"Yep, that was old Willis alright."

Uvalde County Sherriff, Kenneth Kelley, a respected lawman that was elected to serve six terms as county sheriff. Though he arrested Willis Newton several times on minor offences, Willis considered him a friend and confidant. Sherriff Kelley rarely carried a gun while in office.

In reality, the episode cost Willis a great deal more than the $30,000 he bragged that he used as a bribe and tied him up in legal maneuvers that played out over several years. The initial arrest of Willis and his nephew, Neal Oglesby, was reported by the *Ada Evening News* on August 1, 1962. Note the misspelling of Brent's name.

2 Texans Face Kidnap Trial

CLAREMOKE (AP)—Two Texans—Willis Newton, 74, Uvalde, and Neal Oglesby, 45, Corpus Christi—were bound over Tuesday for district court trial on kidnapping charges. They were charged after Frank Breant, Tulsa, was found bound and his mouth taped in the back seat of the Texans' car Thursday night at Claremore.

Breant at first refused to testify at the preliminary hearing but did so on the order of Justice Virgil Purkey. Purkey also made Breant post $2,500 appearance bond for the scheduled trial of the two Texans at the fall term of court.

After Willis, Neal, and Frank all posted bail, the trial was set for district court on October 23. Then through a series of legal maneuvers, the trial was moved to March 25, 1963, as reported by the *Lawton Constitution:*

...Trial has been set for March 25 in Claremore for two Texas men charged with kidnapping.

...Police arrested Newton and Oglesby after officers found Frank Brent tied up with a log chain in the back of their car. Brent told police the men had threatened to throw him into a river. He said Newton had accused him of taking $6,000 in jewelry while he worked for Newton on his ranch near Uvalde.

Shortly before the trial date, Willis was admitted into a San Antonio hospital for arthritis and bursitis. The judge reluctantly rescheduled the trial for April 22. Surprising enough, the trial went to court on that date and in covering the trial the *Lawton Constitution* reported:

...Oglesby asked for and received a separate trial. It will come up on the next jury docket.

Tuesday, Oglesby testified that Brent offered to change his story if Oglesby and Newton would give him $3,000. Oglesby said he met Brent in a Tulsa tavern, last week and discussed the case. He said Brent proposed to "wipe everything out" and leave the area if he could get the money.

Defense attorney R. A. Wilkerson called a San

Antonio waitress Tuesday as the first defense witness. The waitress, Mrs. Alberta Winston, testified that Brent showed her some jewelry that matched the items Newton reported as stolen from his ranch. Mrs. Winston said she met Brent in a club at Castroville, Tex., on Jan. 21, 1962. Brent denied showing her any jewelry,

The trial ended with a hung jury but the state went at Willis again in October of 1963 and this time they convicted him. The *Ada Evening News* covered the jury's decision, with a touching account of Willis crying at the trial.

CLAREMORE (AP)—A District Court jury, which deliberated seven hours Saturday, convicted 74-year-old Willis Newton of kidnapping a man he described as a close friend. The jury found Newton guilty under the lesser of two Oklahoma kidnaping laws and fixed his sentence at a year and a day in prison. It was his second trial on the charge. The stronger law provides punishment of 10 years to death. The law under which Newton was convicted provides for a sentence of up to 10 years.

Newton, of Uvalde, Tex., will remain free on bond pending formal sentencing Nov. 6. He came to court on crutches. He and his nephew, Noel Oglesby, 45, Corpus Christi, Tex., were charged with kidnapping after officers found Frank Brent, 44, Tulsa, bound and gagged in their car last year. Newton was tried last April, but that ended in a hung jury.

...He (Willis) described Brent as a close friend and wept Friday when Brent's testimony about visits to the Newton home was read.

So with trial ending with a conviction of a tearful Willis, the appeal process began with him out on bail. Finally, on September 8, 1965, the Oklahoma Court of Criminal Appeals overruled the conviction when they could not find Frank Brent to testify. In the court record it stated:

...The Tulsa County deputy sheriff testified that two days before the trial commenced he received the first subpoena and went to the residence of the missing witness the following day, but failed to learn of his whereabouts. He then proceeded to inquire at several of the beer halls where Brent frequently visited, but failed to locate him.

The trial court instructed the deputy sheriff to obtain another subpoena and to make another search of Tulsa County. The following day, October 18th, the deputy sheriff testified that he did make a thorough search, with the aid of the Tulsa County sheriff's office, the Tulsa police department, highway patrol, and radio and television, but failed to locate the witness.

...Due diligence implies more than partial notice, and last-minute activities. Had the county attorney been more attentive to the issuance of his subpoenas when the matter was set down for trial, the sheriff would have been provided more opportunity to locate the witness. But, in this case, it is obvious that the search for the witness took place at the last minute, which is not due diligence.

...It is the decision of this Court that the trial court erred in permitting the reading of the transcript of testimony into this record. Therefore, for the reasons stated herein, the case is reversed.

So after spending a small fortune in legal fees and numerous court appearances Willis had beat the rap again. The only unanswered question is—what happened to Frank Brent? Did Willis pay him to leave the state or does his skeletal remains reside at the bottom of a lake chained to an engine block?

Rowena Bank Job

"I'm in Laredo, Texas and I've got a lot of witnesses here. Is anybody looking for me?"

It would seem that Willis, in his mid-70s would call it quits. Well, it just was not in him to crawl up in his rocking chair and drift into obscurity. Not Willis, not by a long shot.

Shortly after midnight on March 1, 1968, Constable Clarence Goetz at the Runnels County Sheriff's office received a phone call from a liquor store in Rowena, Texas. The bank across the street was being robbed. Goetz notified Sheriff Don Atkins and within minutes two squad cars filled with lawmen roared off for Rowena, which was nine miles away from the courthouse in Ballinger. They arrived at the bank and found Doc Newton and another Uvalde man, R.C. Talley, inside the bank.

As they pulled up at the bank, the sheriff and his deputies bailed out of their cars and blasted away at the pair in the bank with rifles and a sub-machine gun. The *San Angelo Standard Times* covered the heist with banner headline:

Rowena Shootout Ends With Arrest

BALLINGER—Bill Doc Newton, 76, of Uvalde and Robert C. Talley, 47, of Del Rio are in Runnels County jail after being charged with the early morning burglary Of Rowena First National Bank, which was interrupted by a volley of gunfire from law officers.

Talley, a rancher who reportedly owns two ranches, is under $25,000 bond while bond on Newton has been denied.

Runnels County Sheriff Don Atkins has issued statewide alerts for a third man believed to have been the driver of a getaway car.

Three men were spotted outside the small bank about 12:30 AM Thursday by Butch Lisso, who notified officers who were on the scene within 12 minutes, surrounding the bank, Adkins, Deputy

Marvin Titsworth, police officers Wayne Bailey and George Barta, Rowena Constable Clarence Goetz and Lisso ordered the men out.

Officers reported seeing three men, two at the door of the bank. Lisso said one man clearly had a riffle. Later it was found the men had two .38 caliber pistols and a 30-30 caliber Winchester rifle.

When lawmen ordered the intruders out, they got a shot as a reply. Atkins moved to the rear door of the bank and opened fire through two doors.

"I guess there were about ten shots fired," said Atkins, "but I'm not positive myself."

After officers returned the fire, one man came out of the bank with his hands up, but the other remained in the bank.

The prisoner told Atkins the other man was armed inside but Adkins, disregarding his own safety, entered the bank's front door armed with a rifle and pistol.

Atkins caught site of the burglar and ordered him to lie down, but the elderly man resisted. Atkins and the man scuffled, and in the struggle the burglar struck his head on a door facing, cutting a gash.

Newton was treated in Ballinger Memorial Hospital after his arrest then transferred to the County jail.

The pistols and a riffle were found inside the bank within easy reach of the burglar.

Both men were taken before Peace Justice D. W. Turner to be charged.

Inside the bank was a stack of papers, burglary tools and near the front door was an auger used to cut a square hole in the door, which the men used to stick their hands through and unlocked the front door.

...The theory of a third man and a getaway car is supported by the fact no heavy cutting equipment or blasting material was uncovered in the lawman's investigation. Lisso said he first thought the men were leaving but he saw them return to the bank, but he did not see a car. For a time lawmen thought a pickup parked in Rowena was the vehicle used by the men but later it was found to be owned by a local farmer.

"I feel like they were making a trip to the car for other necessary tools when we arrived," said Atkins. "We did not find a torch or nitro and they would have had to have them to get into the safe."

Newton who has served time in Leavenworth prison has lived in Uvalde several years.

Talley, who Uvalde officers say lives in Uvalde, has no criminal record. His wife lives in Del Rio.

...Bank president George Ruppert said this is the first attempt at robbing the bank since 1953. No money was lost Thursday nor was any taken in 1953 or 1935 when intruders broke through a wall.

Doc and R.C. Talley took the bank door sign literally when they opened it with a ballpeen hammer, a chisel, and a hand drill.

Finally when the clip on the deputy's Thompson machine gun ran out of bullets and the others stopped shooting, the Rowena First National Bank was a shot up mess. Plate glass windows were shattered and bullet holes riddled the doors and walls of the bank. Within a short time after the shooting had stopped, the bank president arrived on the scene, saw the damage, and became infuriated with the lawmen. The robbers did a small amount of damage to a side door and yet the officers had blasted away at them with a barrage of gunfire.

The First National Bank of Rowena the night of the bungled burglary by the last of the Newton Gang.

The *Abilene Reporter News* provided a better detailed account of the robbery.

> ROWENA—The attempted burglary of the First National Bank here early Thursday and the following shootout, could have been taken from a Western movie. No one was injured in the fusillade of shots, but two men were captured. The pair, Robert C. Talley Jr., 47, of Del Rio, and Bill Newton, 76, of Uvalde, were charged with bank burglary before Justice of the Peace D. W. Turner Jr. at Ballinger.
>
> Police officers said Butch Lisso, who runs a liquor store across the street from the bank,

heard noises coming from the institution about 12:30 a.m. and saw two men breaking into the building. They said he noticed they were armed. It was later learned the two men possessed two .38 pistols .and a lever-action 38-40 Winchester rifle. Lisso called the authorities and the first one to be notified was Constable Clarence Goetz. "When I got the call, I told my wife to load my gun, and I rushed out even forgetting my socks."

Police photograph of the weapons recovered at the robbery scene in Rowena.

The newspaper article continued with Goetz's account of the robbery:

Goetz said when he got near the bank he saw two men walking towards it and assumed they were sheriff's deputies coming to help. "I was standing in the middle of the street so I could see them better. I put the cross hairs of my scope on the two—and I saw it was the burglars!

The burglars had apparently broken into the bank, then left to pick up some burglar tools and were returning with them when Goetz arrived on the scene," he said. As the two entered the bank for the second time, Goetz crouched in the shadows and "held them in his scope," and across the street, Lisso had acquired a rifle, and had it trained on them. "I saw them' enter the bank both times," Lisso said. "I think in all there must have been three, even though I only saw two at a time enter the bank each time. But the second time one of the men looked differently to me".

About this time, according to Goetz, a passing motorist drove by the bank and "spooked" the burglars. "I could tell through my scope they were getting nervous and might try to leave. I could have shot them right there in the bank— but I waited. Then I heard the hum of that police Ford coming fast and I knew things were going to happen."

The police car roared up to the corner where the bank is located and on the well-lighted street in front of the glass doors of the building. Out jumped four police officers and sheriff's men, according to Lisso.

"I was carrying a Thompson sub-machine gun and I went up to the front of the glass doors," said sheriff's deputy Marvin Titsworth. "As I did, I heard them run for the back of the building and that's when the other officers headed them off at the only other door."

The other officers were Ballinger Policemen Wayne Bailey, George Barta, and Sheriff Don Atkins. "We yelled at them to come out with their hands up, but they wouldn't," said Sheriff Atkins. About this time, he said he and Officer Bailey, covered by officer Barta, opened fire on the rear door. They put 15 to 20 rounds through the door.

Deputy Titsworth then said he yelled, "Come on out." He said through the front glass he saw one man walking slowly towards him. "I couldn't see him too well and I told him to put his hands up over his head or I would shoot him," Titsworth said. Talley complied, and once he was out front, he and Atkins handcuffed him face down in front of the bank. "The other fellow was still reluctant!" said Atkins, "so I went after him. About two-thirds of the way back in he stood up behind a counter, and I told him to put his hands up and to lie on the floor". Atkins said the man didn't want to lie down, and a scuffle ensued, and the sheriff had to battle him to the floor. In the scuffle Newton received a minor head injury, the sheriff said.

"The sheriff was taking a terrific chance by going in there," Titsworth said. "The man was wearing coveralls which could have concealed a gun. He was lucky the sheriff didn't shoot him." Officers were unable to find a getaway car. They presumed there may have been a third person involved but that he escaped.

Officer Barta had one comment after it was over. "I just couldn't find a spot dark enough for me on that lighted street," he said. "I was okay while it was going on and even while I was standing in front of that door with a machine gun, but I got a little weak after that fella finally came out and gave himself up," Titsworth said.

Entry to the bank was gained by boring holes around the front door lock with a brace and bit. Besides the weapons, officers also confiscated a bag of burglary tools. About two weeks ago, a shed at the Steak House here was burglarized of tools.

Ballinger police photo of the break-in tools used by Doc Newton and R.C. Talley

Later that same morning of the bank debacle, Sheriff Kenneth Kelley received a phone call at his home in Uvalde. He recalled the events following the Rowena robbery:

"A Ranger called me from Runnels County around 3:00 A.M. and said, 'We got some of your people in jail that was trying to rob a bank.' I said, 'The Newtons?' 'Yeah, how did you know?' 'Well, I saw Willis, R.C. Talley and Doc in Willis's car yesterday, early.'

"I figured they was up to something, but I didn't know what. I told the Ranger that Willis was driving. He said that they did not have Willis there.

"Then a little later that morning Willis called me and says, 'What's this I hear about a bank robbery?'

"I hear they had one.'

"What happened?'

"They caught a couple of men inside the bank.'

"The crazy s.o.b.'s don't they know they can convict them if they catch them inside'? Then Willis says, 'I'm in Laredo, Texas and I've got a lot of witnesses here. Is anybody looking for me?'

"I said, 'Not yet.'

"So then Willis said, 'I'll be back in the morning and I'll call you when I get there.'

"Then the next morning the FBI called me from Del Rio and wanted to know if Willis was in Uvalde. I told them that he had called me and said he would be home sometime that day.

"Then a little later, Willis called me and said he was home. He asked if anyone was looking for him.

"I said 'Yeah, the Del Rio people want to talk to you.' He said, 'Tell them to go to hell!'

"Willis said the only way he would talk to the FBI was if I was with them. But when the FBI finally arrived I had to go out on a call so I couldn't go out there with them to Willis's house.

"So I called out there to his house and convinced him to talk with the lawmen. They went to Willis's house and talked with him for a short while and then he announced, 'This interview is over, you all can leave.'

"The officers left without getting anything from Willis.

"No charges were ever issued for Willis in the robbery. Later, I got indictment papers for Doc and R.C. Tally.

"They were up there at Willis's house so I went up there to serve the papers. They had not made bail but were let out to come back to Uvalde.

"You never heard such cussing and carrying-on at that house—they were angry with a Texas Ranger that had given a story on them to Life Magazine. Doc was pretty used-up from his head knocking. After I served the papers I left and the group continued their cussing."

Chuckling, Sheriff Kelley said that later Willis and Joe came by his office and autographed his copy of *Album of Gunfighters* that featured the Newton Gang among other notorious outlaws.

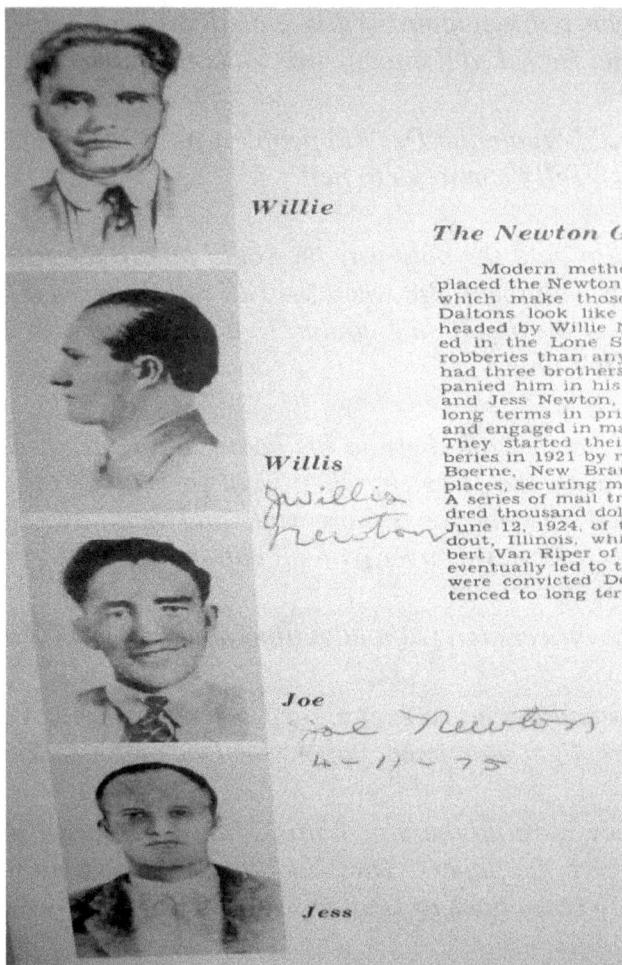

Willie

Willis

Joe

Jess

The Newton G

Modern methc
placed the Newton
which make those
Daltons look like
headed by Willie N
ed in the Lone St
robberies than any
had three brothers
panied him in his
and Jess Newton,
long terms in pris
and engaged in ma
They started their
beries in 1921 by re
Boerne, New Brau
places, securing me
A series of mail tra
dred thousand dol
June 12, 1924, of t
dout, Illinois, whi
bert Van Riper of
eventually led to th
were convicted De
tenced to long terr

Sheriff Kelley's autographed copy of the Newton brothers' page in the
Album of Gunfighters.

The law all knew that Willis was the third man in the robbery but they did not have any hard evidence to convict him so they went to trial with Doc, a near invalid, and R.C. Talley. Though they could not get Willis, the prosecution had no trouble in getting both Doc and R.C. to plead nolo contendere—no contest. Talley got five years and Newton got two years. Both men did their time without admitting that Willis was the third man that got away that night.

Now, in an exclusive interview at age 92, R.C. Talley wanted to set the record straight.

"First off, I want to say that I think Willis Newton was a good man, one of the best men I ever met. He was always giving people money—they would stop him on the street and ask for help and he would give them money.

"I had made a lot of money but then I done lost it all. When my wife left me in '67 I was running a beer joint down in Del Rio and pretty near ran myself into the grave not eating and working without no sleep.

"Finally, I closed up the beer joint and drove to Willis' house in Uvalde. He had to come out and help me get in his house. He saw right away I wasn't going to make it if he couldn't get me out of bed and eating so he worked with me until I recovered.

"After a while I come around and started feeling better. Then one morning I come into the kitchen and saw there wasn't a damn thing to eat. Willis said, 'I ain't got a damned thing, I'm broke. Mammy (Louise) had died and Willis had gone through all of his money.

"Doc was down at another house and he didn't have nothing to eat.

"Willis said, 'We did a little bank last week and didn't get nothing but a little change. We're getting too old, we can't lift them acetylene tanks through the door to burn the safe.' They had robbed several places over in East Texas but they didn't amount to much.

"I was about 49 at the time and I said I would help them rob banks because Willis had saved my life.

"So in a few days we went over to East Texas and around midnight we pulled up on the side of this bank. I unloaded the tanks and put them inside the bank. Then I went back outside and stood in the shadows as a lookout.

Willis and Doc got inside the vault but they couldn't get into the little safe that had all the money so they come dragging the change bags out the side door. That's all we got—about $1,500 in change.

"We pulled out of town about daylight and later I looked down the road and said, 'Willis, we got a big roadblock coming up.' Cool as could be Willis said, 'Well just straighten up real good and we'll be all right.' He was wearing his fancy businessman's clothes and that little hat.

"Damned if we didn't pass right through the law and they never stopped us.

"Right away Willis had spent all the money so he says he has this bank in Rowena; figured it would bring about $40,000. Well, we went up there one night and looked it over and come back to wait for a real cold night to rob the bank.

"Sure enough about a month later we went up there and it was colder than blue hell.

"Willis dropped Doc and me off at the side door of the bank and he went on up the street about two blocks and pulled the Cadillac into a closed up cotton gin where he was going to be the lookout.

"Doc and I had a ballpeen hammer, a chisel, and a hand drill to open the door. I tried drilling through the door but it had a sheet of lead in the middle that stopped the drill bit. So I took the chisel and hammer; I laid into that old-time door latch and finally broke it off. When I did the door come open.

"But the son-of-a bitch was wired and it set off an alarm in the liquor store across the street from the bank.

"So Doc and me went in the bank and started looking around. About that time I heard the echo of sirens outside. I told Doc, 'We got rank (cops).'

"We could hear them cars coming from the Ballinger police. About this time Willis decided he needed a 'bennie' (Benzedrine, an early amphetamine stimulant) to stay alert so he was fumbling around in his trunk looking for his medicine bag when the cops come up the street. He started to come over to us but he heard the cars coming fast so he went back to his car and took off.

"He was going to circle around behind the bank so he could pick us up coming out the side door. I opened the back door about six inches and slammed it shut—the law was already there at the front.

"After I shut the door we backed away from it. About that time that blamed deputy opened up on it with a machine gun. Shot it to pieces and me and Doc was standing against the wall with bullets whizzing ever which way.

"We went to the front and there was a deputy with another machine gun at the front door. So we throwed our guns on the counter and the sheriff broke through the door and said to lay down on the floor.

"Doc was a little bit slow getting down because of his knees so that damn crazy sheriff came up and hit him on the head with a gun butt. I could feel the warm blood spilling down that cold floor;

"I thought that Doc was dead. That same guy that busted Doc run up to me, put a gun to my head and said, 'If you move, I'll shoot your head off!'

"About that time the man who owned the bank rode up. He was hollering, 'Get the hell out of my bank!' He was

hollering and a cussing that Ballinger sheriff for shooting up his bank. That sheriff was plumb crazy. I think he would have killed Doc and me if that banker hadn't showed up.

"They handcuffed me and took me over to Ballinger. An ambulance came and picked up Doc. Willis got away in the Cadillac and nobody stopped him.

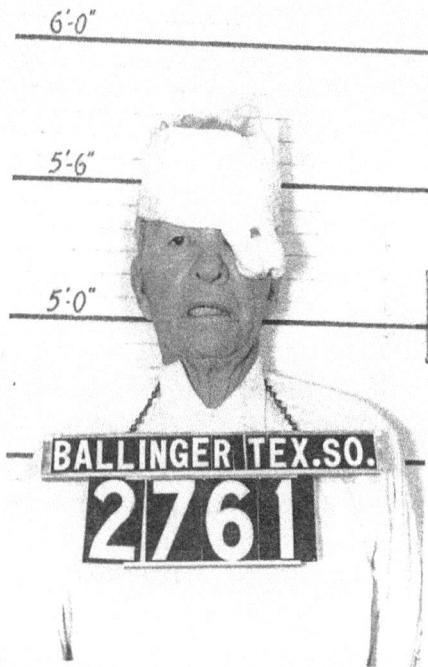

Police booking mug shot of Doc Newton with a heavily bandaged head wound on the night of the Rowena bank burglary.

Continuing R.C. Talley's account:

"That little 'ol court appointed lawyer told me that they was going to give me 12 years if we went to trial so he was going to cut a deal with the judge.

"Finally he come back and said they'd give me five years but I would only have to serve one year if we didn't go to trial. They let me see my boy, Josh, in the courtyard. When I come back in I said, 'I'll go for the deal."

Willis Newton at the trial for his brother Doc and R.C. Talley. Note the dapper coat and hat along with his trademark Cadillac.

"Willis and my daddy came down to see me twice while I was in the pen but I wouldn't talk to them 'cause I was mad at them. They didn't do a damn thing for me while I was in jail.

When I got out Willis said, 'Kid, I just couldn't do nothing because I was out of money.'"

R.C. Talley in his easy chair at his home in Uvalde, Texas.

Given that Willis was an accomplished liar, definitely on a par with the best Chicago politician at a press conference, he swore that he had nothing to do with the Rowena robbery until the day he died. R.C. Talley outlived everybody to finally set the record straight.

Death of the Newton Gang

With the exception of R.C. Talley and "Little Joe" Newton, all of the members of the Newton Gang are buried in the Hillcrest Memorial Park Cemetery in Uvalde. It is interesting to note that Joe Newton and his wife are buried in a separate burial spot from the others.

As it played out, the Newtons outlived all of the other major players in the Rondout robbery. Although he was never indicted, **Dean O'Banion** was the first to depart when the beer runner was rubbed out by hired torpedoes on the morning of November 10, 1924. Ironically O'Banion was clipping chrysanthemums in the back room of a funeral parlor.

On October 11, 1926, **Earl J. Weiss (Hymie "the Polack")** and some of his pals were crossing the street to the Holy Name Cathedral in Chicago. They never made it; a gunman threw the bolt back on a Thompson machine gun and then with a tug on the trigger, started spewing .45 bullets from a 50-round drum clip. It continued until the 39th shell jammed in the firing chamber. Weiss was hit 10 times before he crashed to the sidewalk. He died en route to the hospital.

Then in 1931 **Herbert Holliday** was the next to bite the dust. After giving up all of his buried loot, he was released from prison after only doing six years. Within a month, he had organized a gang and tried to steal a set of automobile tires on June 12, 1931. Two American Express agents shot and killed Holliday before he could get away. A rather inglorious ending (stealing tires) for someone who had been part of the biggest train robbery in American history.

James (The Fixer) Murray was released on parole in 1937 and returned to Chicago, Illinois. He immediately resumed his criminal operations. Then late one night he had left a tavern and was waiting for a streetcar. He saw a black Buick pull up to the curb. From inside, one of the men motioned to him and hollered, "Hey buddy, come over here. We want to talk with you." Murray went over and leaned into the window on the passenger side. Two .38 slugs in his face later he was a goner.

Brent Glasscock became a model prisoner and worked hard to rehabilitate himself. Postal inspectors visited him several times trying to find out where more of the missing loot was hidden. Glasscock never divulged the location of any remaining loot and was released in 1937. At this point it is thought that he moved out to California and quietly faded into obscurity.

Newspaper clipping showing Postmaster General Harry S. New holding the gun given to him by Brent Glasscock after he was sent to prison. Rush D. Simmons, chief of the post-office inspectors is on the left. Simmons led the team that captured the gang that robbed the Rondout train in 1924.

William (Bill) Fahy continued to protest his innocence, but he turned down opportunities for parole. He was eventually released from prison in 1937. Through his "Chicago Irish Connections," he was hired as a claims investigator on the Chicago Surface Lines (go figure). He died in 1943.

Jess Newton

Jess died of lung cancer at the age of 83 in a VA hospital in Temple, Texas. The date was March 4, 1960. His tombstone reflects that he had been a member of the Texas Brigade in WWI.

After leaving the wild times working for Willis in Tulsa, Jess returned to Texas to do what he knew best—ranch work. He had eased back on his drinking and as a result, became known to the Uvalde ranchers as a dependable ranch hand. Hayden Haby, a local rancher, grew up with "Little Joe" Newton and was around Jess frequently when he worked for Hayden's father.

> *"One of the best meals I ever ate was jackrabbit stew cooked in a Dutch oven over a campfire by Jess Newton." Haby recalled in an interview. "Jess was good help, I remember one time he helped us drive cattle to the railroad stock pens in Spofford. It wasn't that far from where his brother Willis robbed his first train."*

On an earlier occasion, when Haby was a young boy, he remembered Jess had driven up to the Haby ranch in a real nice car. Sitting beside him was a beautiful Indian woman. They visited for a while and then drove off. Haby said that Jess never married the woman.

Then later Haby said his mother, Sara, told him that Jess had told her that he had lost $75,000 in a liquor store when it burned in Galveston. That would probably coincide with the firebombing of Willis's joint on Mustang Island but when asked; Haby did not known whether Willis was involved.

According to Haby, Jess never hesitated in talking about the Rondout robbery and his escape to Mexico. After crossing the border, Jess said he signed up with the Mexican government to fight Poncho Villa's rebels. He said that they went to take a little village down there and a bandit sentry spotted them, jumped up and starting running back to town. Jess and the Mexican troops started shooting at the man and although they could see the hair flying up on the back of the man's head, he kept running until he was out of sight. The next day they found the man—alive, but badly wounded. Jess left the Mexican forces a short time later.

Jess said the law was trying to lure him back across the border. One old tough got to drinking with Jess and he said there was a wild horse over in Del Rio that nobody could ride. Jess took the challenge.

As Jess and the other man walked across the bridge the man slapped handcuffs on Jess and said he was under arrest. Jess said, "Well you son of a bitch I would have never believed."

When asked about the missing buried loot, Haby chuckled and said,

"Jess never told where he hid the money but when he would run low on money in North Uvalde he would tell someone that 'he had a mare and colt down at La Pryor and I need to go down there to check on them.'

"He would ask someone to drive him down there. Jess would get out, be gone awhile, and come back. He said the horses were just fine and then he would be in the chips for a while."

Haby smiled and then said, "¿quién sabe?"

Jess' missing Rondout loot, which he supposedly buried in an alcoholic state outside San Antonio, was never found. Willis was sure he knew where it was buried—somewhere out toward Bandera but he was not exactly sure of the spot.

Wylie (Doc) Newton

Doc Newton died of cancer on September 27, 1974, in the Uvalde Memorial Hospital at the age of 83. He had lingered in a nursing home since he returned from prison.

Willis' "wolf bit" brother could barely hobble around his mother's old house in North Uvalde before he died. The bullet wounds, beatings and the final "pistol whipping" he suffered in the Rowena debacle had finally caught up with Doc Newton.

In an interview Willis talked about his brother:

"When Doc got out Leavenworth, he went to farming down in Oklahoma. After about 12 years he sold the place and moved him and his wife over to an apartment in Oklahoma City. She got a job in a packing plant and Doc fooled around hauling cattle, never making much money.

"After about three years, he moved to Tulsa where I paid him $200 a day running whiskey from Joplin, Missouri. Then he got to drinking that whiskey and pretty soon the law was on to him so he had to quit. So I give him some money and told him to go back to Oklahoma City.

"Doc's wife divorced him so he left Oklahoma City and come down here to Texas. Got down here and didn't do a damned thing! Then he and R.C. Talley got arrested for trying to rob that Rowena bank. That's where that crazy sheriff 'pistol whipped' him! Hell, Doc was 76 years old and he hit him in the head with a pistol!

"When he was younger he had worked as an iron worker down at Corpus Christi for about five years. He made good money and paid a bunch into Social Security, but dammed if they didn't give him just $200 month to live on when he was 65."

The *San Angelo Standard Times* interviewed Doc when he was in jail awaiting trial for the Rowena bank robbery. The article quoted Doc as saying:

> *"I have had my last fling,' Newton said Monday, adding he was glad to submit to an interview. 'Although I doubt I will be around long enough to read it.*
>
> *"But I am trying to do what is right. If I had my life to live over, it would be far different.'*
>
> *"My heart is almost gone. I have been shot up in so many places that I have arthritis in my hands and legs.' Officers in Sheriff Don Adkins office took Newton to the office of a doctor here Monday for a checkup*
>
> *"Newton discounted the injury but said, 'I have terrible headaches. They sometimes affect my memory, but I have quick recall at most times for an old man.'*
>
> *"The grandfatherly looking subject has a kindly face, though it is battle-scarred. In the Illinois robbery, he was shot in the hand, jaw, shoulder and twice in the side.*
>
> *"...Of the Runnels County officers, he said, 'I hold no grudge toward them. They have a job to do; it is dangerous and they did it well.'"*

So in some regards, it appears that old Doc finally did seek repentance from his outlaw life. It might be worth noting that the pastor of Northside Baptist Church conducted his funeral.

Joe Newton

The youngest of the Newton brothers, Joe died 10 years after Willis. He had dealt with a number of health problems but finally died on February 2, 1989 at the age of 88 in the Uvalde hospital.

Following his release from the McAlester prison in Oklahoma in 1946, Joe returned to Uvalde and played it straight for the rest of his long life. He started out as a $35 a month ranch hand, then worked at breaking wild horses and ultimately went into the hide hunting business. In the process he managed to earn enough to purchase a meat market and then later a drive-in café. While Willis was still dreaming up schemes to make "easy money," Joe stayed true to the pledge he made to his wife that he would earn money the "hard way" in legitimate enterprises.

He did slip once and, though it did not cost him a run-in with the law, he paid a stiff price to be reminded by his wife that "easy money" was only a fool's dream. Many years later his son, "Little Joe", quoted his dad as saying, "It must have been the medicine I was taking for my neck pain or it was just plain stupidity."

In the late 1960s, Joe fell for the classic scam-game, the "pigeon drop." He was in downtown San Antonio and was approached by a black man claiming to have found an envelope containing a large sum of money. The black man (serving as the roper) steered him to an accomplice (a white man). He convinced Joe to return to Uvalde to provide some "earnest money" so all three could split the booty. Joe went to the drugstore where his wife worked and asked for the keys to the safety deposit box so he could cash in some certificates of deposit. He told his wife he was "working a deal" which she took to mean a cattle deal. Wrong. Without a moment of hesitation, Joe handed the man $13,000 and agreed to a meeting place to split the windfall. He never saw the money or the con artist again.

Otherwise, Joe led an exemplary life in his hometown and though known as an ex-bank robber he was well received by all that knew him and they were more than willing to buy him a cup of coffee at the drugstore fountain. In his later years he finally submitted to interviews and talking about his outlaw years. Though it made a good story to tell, he did not relish being remembered as an outlaw. He preferred to being known for his skill with horses. When asked how wanted to be remembered, he did not hesitate.

> *"Being a bronc rider, I guess. When I rode a bad horse, everybody used to come around and watch me ride, but now everybody is dead that ever seen me ride a horse. I was never throwed in my life and I never got hold of the horn in my life on a pitching horse. I would have been better off staying there instead of going off and robbing banks.*
>
> *"I was a damn fool for doing it. I could have owned a big piece of Texas if I hadn't got into it. I was a cowboy. I was working and saving my money to go to the Big Bend. Hell, you could buy land out there for a dollar an acre back then."*

He certainly gave the impression that he regretted what he had done with Willis and that unlike his brother, stopped thinking like a criminal.

Willis Newton

Willis died 20 years after his wife, Louise passed away. Joe took Willis into the hospital in Uvalde where they ran a series of tests and then he was transferred to a San Antonio hospital where he died on August 22, 1979.

Willis Newton—outlaw to the very end.

Ex-Uvalde County Sheriff Kenneth Kelley said that Willis Newton always seemed to have plenty of money. According to Kelley, Willis maintained close ties to his criminal brotherhood and never gave up his life of crime. "He apparently had people all over the country," Kelley said. "He'd case a location and a few days later it would get robbed."

Kelley related that Willis went along with R.C. Talley's dad to visit his son in prison at Huntsville.

"When they left, they went by some little town that way and pulled up in front of the bank. Willis sat there and

229

looked at it for a while and then said to Mr. Talley, 'I believe we can take this thing now—I got run away from here once before.' A little after that, it come out in the Texas Lawman News that that bank had been hit by burglars. Whether it was Willis or not—I don't know.

"The next time they rode down to the prison they came back by a different direction and Willis stopped at a big, fancy house set back from the road with a chained entrance. Willis stopped, backed up and then got out and walked up to the front door. He knocked at the front door and when nobody answered he walked around the house knocking on every door. Finally he came back to the car and said, 'There's a million dollars' worth of antiques in there. I guess I had better get hold of some of the boys.' Later, it came out in the lawmen's bulletin that the house had been burglarized."

However, Kelley also remembered that the winter before Willis died; he knocked on his door one night and asked to borrow a small electric heater to keep from freezing. "It looked like all his money had played out."

Joe Newton tried to care for his brother when "all of his money had played out." On most mornings before Willis' death, Joe and R.C. Talley would gather at Willis' house for morning coffee with the nearly-invalid gang leader. Later, when Joe was interviewed, he recalled Willis' unbending attitude.

"You can do those things for a while, but you can't keep on doing them. We were crazy. No way in the world anyone with any sense would do anything like that ...but Willis didn't really believe in stopping, not until the day he died."

Hillcrest Memorial Park Cemetery in Uvalde, Texas

When you walk through the Hillcrest Memorial Park Cemetery in Uvalde and pass through the line of gravestones it is easy to overlook the common sounding family name of Newton—especially the dual grave marker, **NEWTON – J. Willis & Louise M**. Without knowing the story it would be hard to fathom that interred beneath that marker was the leader of the infamous Newton Gang and his wife.

Today, very few people remember the name, Willis Newton, or that of his outlaw brothers. While the exploits of other western outlaws are still the grist of books and movies, Willis and his gang have largely been forgotten and literally buried in that cemetery on the edge of town. Yet when you compare their criminal careers with the James brothers, the Daltons, the Youngers, Billy the Kid, Sam Bass, and the other outlaws of the 19th century there is no comparison; the Newtons robbed more banks and trains than all of the others combined. The same holds true for the outlaws of the early 20th century—Bonnie and Clyde, "Baby Face" Nelson, John Dillinger, "Machine Gun" Kelly, Ma Barker and "Pretty Boy" Floyd. All were romanticized in breathless newspaper accounts, lurid books and sensational movies. Yet, taken as a whole, they could not match the Newtons in the number of robberies committed nor total loot taken.

The difference in notoriety lies in the fact that the Newtons did not have a string of dead bodies following in their wake. Willis had counted on that fact to dodge the law throughout his 75 year criminal career. Even though it was not completely true, he took great pride in saying that he and his brothers had never killed anyone.

> *"I use to tell everyone; don't shoot nobody unless you have to. If you have to shoot, make it where you won't kill them. Once you kill somebody, you're in real trouble because they'll hunt you down. You can count on it."*

Willis' twisted sense of morality can probably be traced to his mother who raised her brood on heroic stories of the outlaws of the Old West. Add to that the general distrust of the government and law officers in general; Willis could justify his actions as simply taking what he wanted from the "the bigger thieves—bankers and insurance companies."

In some ways, it might have been fitting for his tombstone to have this inscription added:

"Why if you don't get caught, then you're innocent!"

232

Epilogue

A few weeks before Willis Newton died he was admitted to the hospital in Uvalde, Texas for tests on a multitude of physical problems. After he had been there a several days I went by his room and visited the old outlaw. I knocked on his door and he managed a weak, "Come on in."

When I entered his room I saw a very emaciated version of what I had seen in March of that year. Rail thin and covered with a crimson rash on his legs, Willis cocked his head sideways and demanded, "Who are you?"

I politely reminded him that we had talked at his home earlier and that he had given me advice on robbing banks and trains. He nodded his head and stared up at the ceiling, "Yeah, I remember now."

I told him I was sorry to see him ailing and in pain. He responded by saying, "Yeah, I'm headed to the bar ditch. The doctor says everything's gone crazy inside of me. I know I'm a goner and wish I could kill myself but I can't, 'cause I still got my mind. Only crazy people kill themselves but I ain't crazy."

Realizing that his time was about up I asked him if he had any regrets or was sorry for anything he had done in his life. He cocked his head sideways and raised his head up off of the pillow glaring at me. "Hell no," he screeched at me. "I'd still be doing them things but my body's done played out on me. If I was 20 years younger I'd be running guns across the border into Mexico and bringing drugs back! Nobody's ever give me nothing but hell and I ain't ashamed of anything I done!"

So much for contrition and redemption.

I did not know how to respond and remained quiet. After a moment he stared at the ceiling again and added, "The only thing I'm sorry about is that $200,000 those cowards left in that bank when they got spooked. They said, 'We've got $65,000 in bonds and we're getting out before we get caught.' Hell, we left $200,000 just sitting there on that counter. Damn shame, I told them I always wanted it all!"

The next day they moved Willis to a hospital in San Antonio where he died on August 22, 1979. Fierce and defiant to the bitter end he died the way he had lived—as an outlaw.

Even with Willis' expert help, the paper-back Western I managed to write was an unmitigated disaster. For a period of time I gave up writing but a few years later I moved into writing screenplays trying to get some of what Willis called, "Hollywood money." After writing a small number of Western scripts that won writing awards but were not made into movies I gave up writing once again.

Then I wrote the dual biographies of two little known gunfighters and their untimely murders in San Antonio. The book was a success and I considered writing Willis' story. At the time I interviewed Willis in Uvalde I was working with the wife of Joe Newton. She was a sweet, genteel woman that spoke softly and was adamant about not discussing her husband's past. Out of respect to her I never interviewed Joe Newton and swore I would never write about Willis Newton and his brothers while she was still alive. Joe's widow passed away a number of years ago and is buried next to her husband in the Uvalde cemetery.

When I decided to write about Willis, I called Joe's only son, Joe Edward Newton and asked if he would tell me about Willis. He agreed and provided me with essential points in the story that I had been unable to nail down. I explained that I had not written anything before now out of respect for his mother. He thanked me for that and gave his permission to use his information in the book.

I also interviewed ex-Sheriff Kenneth Kelley who provided me with a number of first-hand accounts of his dealings with Willis Newton. The Tulsa kidnapping story was my favorite—the way Kelley told the story I could just picture old Willis in the back seat of his Cadillac twisting that chain around Frank Brent's neck trying to get him to confess to stealing his "big diamond."

In addition, I interviewed Hayden Grissin Haby who is one of the premier goat ranchers in the Uvalde area. He went to school with Joe Newton's son, Joe Edward, and knew Jess Newton as a ranch hand on the family ranch when they ran cattle.

To follow up on the varying accounts of how Jess Newton was captured when he fled to Mexico after the Rondout robbery I interviewed the grandson of Texas Ranger Harrison Hamer. Having the same name as his grandfather, Harrison was able to clear up the details of the border arrest and provide me with a factual newspaper account of the incident. He also allowed me to use the splendid photograph of his grandfather.

During my 1979 interview with Willis he went into great detail about the times he had spent in jail or prison. In describing his first prison time he said, "I was jailed for 22 months and 26 days and then sent to Rusk (prison) for two years. Every son of a bitch knowed I was innocent. They knowd I didn't break no law!" Then over the years he spent over 20 years incarcerated in some type of penal confinement. I never got to ask him the question: was it worth it?

My guess the answer would have been a resounding, "Hell yes!"

Spending a fourth of your 90 years of life behind bars hardly seems worth it to me.

As I left Willis Newton's hospital room for the last time I spotted his physician who was a personal friend of mine. I asked him about Willis' condition and he confirmed what I had been told by the dying man. Then with a twinkle in his eye he asked if I wanted to see an X-ray of Willis' spine.

Sure, I had no idea what to expect.

We went to a nearby viewing room and he slapped a film on the lighted viewing board. There was a very distinct spot located near the spinal column. "That's a German Luger slug he's been carrying around for about 30 years. Some old boy shot him up in Oklahoma."

As I gazed at the image, the physician concluded by saying, "And damned if that old outlaw isn't going to be buried with it!"

I guess you could say it was a fitting eulogy—of sorts.

Willis Newton

Acknowledgments

It seems rather strange that I should start by acknowledging a career criminal for the genesis of this book but it is true. If old Willis Newton had not agreed to visit with me and my tape recorder in 1979 I would never attempted to tell his complete story. Though it was just a few months before he passed away, he was still full of vinegar and defending all of his actions throughout his life. As a result, I recorded a heavily biased account of what happened during his days as an outlaw.

To give a more balanced story I decided I had to track down other accounts of the actual events in his life, which led me to a long, protracted research project. There are a large number of people I need to thank for making this book possible.

As I was writing the book I had the opportunity to interview R.C. Talley at his home in Uvalde, Texas. Mr. Talley spent 15 months in the Huntsville State Prison for his involvement in the 1968 botched bank job in Rowena, Texas. He was able to give me detailed accounts of Willis Newton as well as Willis' role in the bank robbery. At the time of his interview Mr. Talley was 92 years old and more than willing to talk to me.

I would like to thank ex-Sherriff Kenneth Kelley for a heavily detailed personal interview at his place in Uvalde. His account of the Rowena bank job and Willis' kidnapping episode in Oklahoma are priceless.

In addition, I would like to thank Joe Edward Newton, the son of Joe Newton, for his candid personal interview at his home in Uvalde. He provided an excellent description of his dad's activities in hunting for gold in Mexico, in Oklahoma and his latter life in Uvalde.

Hayden Grissin Haby was able to shed some light on Jess, Tull and Joe Newton during a taped interview we did a number of years ago.

Harrison Hamer told me stories about his grandfather, Texas Ranger Harrison Hamer, as well as his great uncle, Frank Hamer and the role that they played in capturing Jess Newton at the time he was hiding out in Mexico following the Rondout robbery. He supplied the

236

newspaper sources covering the capture and allowed me to use the picture of his grandfather.

Phil Housel (fullhouseproductions.net) played a major role in snagging my many blunders and did a great job of copy editing the rough draft. It was a pleasure working with him.

I would like to personally thank Dana Gore, the jailer in Ballinger, and Runnels County Sheriff, Bill Baird for their help in covering the Rowena bank robbery.

Other people that offered their help were ex-Texas Ranger Joe Davis, Alan Carmichael, Claude Stanush and Jane Brummett. Fred Egloff, here in Kerrville, provided a rare, out-of-print book on the Rondout robbery.

In addition, I owe a debt of gratitude to a large number of librarians that helped me track down newspaper and other accounts of the Newton Gang. Frank Faulkner at the San Antonio Library and Virginia Davis and Belia Romo at the El Progresso Library in Uvalde were especially generous in lending their research assistance.

Finally, my wife, Jean, deserves special recognition for her diligence in flagging errors in the final drafts. She is truly gifted in spotting sentencing gaffs. Some men get lucky when they choose a partner—I know I sure did.

GRW

Citations

The Early Years

Author's interview with Willis Newton
Brownwood Bulletin, 3-5-1919
Galveston Daily News, 3-17-1919
Galveston Daily News, 3-6-1919
Galveston Daily News, 3-7-1919
San Antonio Express, 3-17-1919

First Bank Hold-Up

Author's interview with Willis Newton
"Most Daring Bandit in American History." The Washington Times, July 20, 1902
Stanush, Claude and David Middleton. The Portrait of an Outlaw Gang. State House Press, 1994.

Son of a Cyclone Farmer

Author's interview with Willis Newton
Daily News staff, "The last American desperado" NYDailyNews.com. Sunday, June 17, 2007.
"Most Daring Bandit in American History." The Washington Times, July 20, 1902.
Stanush, Claude and David Middleton. The Portrait of an Outlaw Gang. State House Press, 1994.

Brothers

Author's interview with Willis Newton
Notice of Newton brothers release from jail. Zavala County Sentinel newspaper – September 9, 1909.
Walker, Donald R. Penology for Profit: A History of the Texas Prison System, 1867–1912 College Station: Texas A&M University Press, 1988.
Biffle, Kent "'Damn Fool' Robber Recalls Years On The Lam" Dallas Morning News June 03, 1985.
Lindee, Susan. Newton Has No Regrets About His Outlawed Days. San Antonio Express News – June 20, 1980
LeRoux, Charles. "Joe Newton, Last of the Outlaws." Toledo Blade, April 5, 1981
Stanush, Claude and David Middleton. The Portrait of an Outlaw Gang. State House Press, 1994.

The Banks

Author's interview with Willis Newton
Author's interview with R.C. Tally
Finley, Larry. "Wounded Rondout Schoolgirl Carried Train Robbery Bullet for Rest of Her Life. Girl was shot on way to school as historic heist of 1924 played out." Sun-Times News Group newsunonline.com – Friday, July 13, 2007
Biffle, Kent "'Damn Fool` Robber Recalls Years On The Lam" Dallas Morning News June 03, 1985.
Lindee, Susan. Newton Has No Regrets About His Outlawed Days. San Antonio Express News – June 20, 1980
LeRoux, Charles. "Joe Newton, Last of the Outlaws." Toledo Blade, April 5, 1981
"The last American desperado" Daily News staff, NYDailyNews.com. Sunday, June 17, 2007.
"Two Spencer Banks Robbed Today." Linton Daily Citizen – November 6, 1923.
"No Trace Found of Bank Bandits." Connersville News – Examiner November 7, 1923.
"San Marcos Robbery Laid to Newton Gang." San Antonio Express – August 17, 1924.
"Newton Gang Hit Sam Marcos." Southwest Texas New Service, San Marcos, Texas.
"Most Daring Bandit in American History." The Washington Times, July 20, 1902.
"Yeggs Rob Hondo Banks." Hondo Anvil Herald Jan. 12, 1921.
"Robber Heel May Lead to Arrest." The Galveston Daily News – January 11, 1921.
Rios, J. A. "Hondo Bank Robbery." History of Medina County.
"Sleuths Strike Snag in Search for Bandits." San Antonio Evening News – February 14, 1921.
"Boerne Citizens State Bank History." Boerne Public Library files.
"Boerne Bank Is Robbed of Bonds." The Galveston Daily News – February 9, 1921.
"Zeitung Version of 1922 Bank Robbery Here Told." New Braunfels Herald, July 19, 1973
Hass, Oscar. "Role of Texas Rangers in City's History Recalled." New Braunfels Herald, New Braunfels, Texas – July 12, 1973.
Goff, Myra Lee Adams. "1922: A Bank Robbery in Downtown New Braunfels." Sophienburg Museum & Archives. New Brunfels., Texas.
"Has $100,000 Insurance." Associated Press Report – March 10, 1922.
"Officers Searched Hills for $100,000 Loot And Robbers." Associated Press

Release – March 10, 1922.
Stanush, Claude and David Middleton. The Portrait of an Outlaw Gang. State House Press, 1994.
Bandits Burn Auto In Eluding Pursuit by Toronto Police. Associated Press – July 25, 1923.
Murderous Holdup of Bank Messengers Is Staged in Toronto. Denton Record Chronicle - July 24, 1923.
"Bandits Burn Auto In Eluding Pursuit by Toronto Police." Associated Press – July 25, 1923.
"Bandits Escape With $130,000." The Moberly Weekly Monitor, July 26, 1923.
"Bandits Get Away." The Lethbridge Daily Herald, July 25, 1923.
"Bandits Kill Bank Messenger." The Moberly Weekly Monitor, July 26, 1923.
"Bandits Shoot Messengers in Street Holdup." Appleton Post-Crescent, Appleton, Wisconsin, July 24, 1923.
"Car Used by Toronto Bank Bandits Found." Manitoba Free Press, July 30, 1923.
"Murderous Holdup of Bank Messengers Is Staged in Toronto." Denton Record Chronicle - July 24, 1923.
"Thinks He Ran Across Toronto Bank Bandits." Manitoba Free Press, July 27, 1923.
"Toronto Bank Robbery Loss Put at $125,000." Manitoba Free Press, July 25, 1923.
"Large Band of Robbers Blow Two Indiana Banks." The Livingston Daily Sun – November 7, 1923.
"Offer $10,000 Reward For Toronto Bandits; Canadian Officials Believe Gang Reached Buffalo -- Wounded Messenger Recovering." New York Times, July 24, 1923
Bandits Get $130,000In A Raid On Toronto; Shoot 4 On Streets; ; Six Highwaymen in Car Rout Fourteen Bank Messengers -- Two May Die. New York Times, July 25, 1923
Emporia Gazette, 11-23-1922
Joplin Globe, 11-24,-1922
Joplin Globe, 11-25-1922
Lawrence Journal World, 11-23-1922
Moberly Evening Democrat, 11-23-1922
Moberly Evening Democrat, 11-30-1922
Moberly Monitor Index, 11-23-1922
Moberly Monitor Index, 11-27-1922
New Castle News, 19-9-1922
Sandusky Register 22-24-1922
Connersville News-Examiner, 11-7-1923
Decatur Daily Democrat, 11-6-1923

Linton Daily Citizen, 11-6-1923
Owne County Democrat, 11-8-1923
Shoal News, 11-7-1923
Washington Democrat, 11-6-1923
Appleton Post-Crescent July 24,1923
Lethbridge Daily Herald - July 25, 1923 - page 1 & 3
Manitoba Free Press July 23, 1923 - page 1 & 2
Manitoba Free Press July 26, 1923
Moberly Weekly Monitor July 25, 1923
Moberly Weekly Monitor July 26, 1923
Winnipeg Free Press - July 25 1923 -page 1 & 4
Winnipeg Free Press - July 27 1923 -page 1 &7
Winnipeg Free Press - July 30 1923 -page 1 & 4

The Trains

Author's interview with Willis Newton
Author's interview with R.C. Tally
Author's interview with Grissin Haby
"Bandits Hold Up Fast Dixie Flyer; Secure Only $400." Decatur Daily Review. November 8, 1921.
Laredo Times 1-8-1915
Denison - Bells Train Robbery
Brownsville Herald, 10-4-1921
Corsicana Daily Sun, 8-26-1921
Galveston Daily News, 8-25-1921
Mexia Evening News, 8-25-1921
San Antonio Light, 8-25-1921
San Antonio Light, 8-26-1921
Texarkana Train Robbery
Galveston Daily News, 9-7-1921
Port Arthur Daily News, 9-7-1921
San Antonio Light, 9-7-1921
Paxton Train Robbery
Carbondale Free Press, 11-8-1921
Carbondale Free Press, 11-9-1921
Edwardsville Intelligencer, 11-8-1921
Mt. Vernon Reporter News, 11-8-1921
Port Arthur Daily News, 11-8-1921
St. Joseph Train Robbery
Joplin Globe, 12-8-1922
Moberly Evening Democrat, 1922
Rondout Train Robbery

Alton Evening Telegraph 11-18-1924
Alton Evening Telegraph 11-25-1924
Alton Evening Telegraph 6-18-1924
Alton Evening Telegraph 6-21-1924
Alton Evening Telegraph 8-27-1924
Bakersfield Morning Echo 6-13-1924 page 1 & 2
Billings Gazette 6-14-1924 page 1 & 2
Bluefield Daily Telegraph 1-3-1925
Bradford Era 4-13-1925
Carbondale Free Press 11-25-1924
Carbondale Free Press 6-13-1924
Carbondale Free Press 6-14-1924
Carbondale Free Press 6-16-1924
Carbondale Free Press 6-17-1924
Carbondale Free Press 8-27-1924
Daily Globe 12-31-1925
Daily Herald 7-4-1924 page 1 & 10
Daily Herald 9-5-1924
Davenport Democrat and Leader 6-13-1924
Decatur Daily Review 11-12-1924
Decatur Daily Review 11-13-1924
Decatur Daily Review 11-14-1924
Decatur Daily Review 11-18-1924.
Decatur Daily Review 11-21-1924
Decatur Daily Review 11-25-1924
Decatur Daily Review 11-5-1924
Decatur Daily Review 12-6-1924
Decatur Daily Review 6-13-1924
Decatur Daily Review 6-19-1924
Decatur Daily Review 6-21-1924
Decatur Daily Review 6-22-1924
Decatur Daily Review 8-27-1924
Decatur Daily Review 8-29-1924
Edwardsville Intelligencer 6-19-1924
Edwardsville Intelligencer 6-19-1924
Edwardsville Intelligencer 7-8-1924
Edwardsville Intelligencer 8-27-1924
Edwardsville Intelligencer 8-27-1924 page 1 & 2
Edwardsville Intelligencer 8-28-1924
Elyria Chronicle Telegram 6-14-1924
Fayette County Leader 11-27-1924
Galveston Daily News 12-13-1924
Gettysburg Times 6-18-1924

Harrison Times 4-24-1925
Indianapolis Star 6-14-1924 page 1 & 9
Indianapolis Star 6-18-1924
Indianapolis Star 6-19-1924 page 1 & 2
Iola Daily Register 11-15-1924
Iola Daily Register 11-29-1924
Iowa City Press Citizen 12-02-1924
Joplin globe 11-20-1924
Joplin globe 12-12-1924
Joplin globe 6-11-1925
Joplin globe 6-13-1924 page 1 & 2
Joplin globe 6-14-1924
Kokomo Tribune 12-17--1924 Yellow Kid
Kokomo Tribune 6-13--1924 page 1 & 16
Laurel Daily Leader 6-16-1924
Logansport Pharos Tribune 12-15-1925
Louise freed Alton Evening Telegraph 9-8-1924
Lowell Sun 8-27-1924
Murphysboro Daily Independent 6-14-1924
Murphysboro Daily Independent 8-29-1924
National Star July -1974
Nevada State Journal 11-18-1924
New Castle News 2-4-1925
New Castle News 8-27-1924 page 1& 9
Ogden Standard Examiner 11-10-1924
Riverdale Pointer 11-28-1924
Riverdale Pointer 1-16-1925
San Antonio Express 1-3-1925
San Antonio Express 2-26-1925
San Antonio Express 4-17-1925
San Antonio Express 7-30-1924
San Antonio Express 8-27-1924 page 1& 3
San Antonio Light 1-1-1925
Steubenville Herald 8-27-1924
Steubenville Herald 8-28-1924
National Star July -1974
Thomasville Times Enterprises 2-14-1925
Titusville Herald 1-3-1925
Traverse City Record Eagle 11-25-1924
Tucson Daily Citizen 10-1-1925
Washington Post 8-28-1924
Waterloo Evening Courier 8-27-1924
Waterloo Evening Courier 8-27-1924 page 1 &2

G.R. Williamson

Wisconsin Rapids Daily Tribune 11-18-1924
Wisconsin Rapids Daily Tribune 11-29-1924
Wisconsin Rapids Daily Tribune 3-25-1925

The Latter Years

Leavenworth

Author's interview with Willis Newton

Tulsa

Author's interview with Willis Newton
Author's interview with R.C. Tally
Author's interview with Joe Edward Newton
Ada Weekly News 10-2-1949
Ada Weekly News 10-6-1949
Ada Weekly News 9-22-1949
Billings Gazette 6-14-1949
Miami Daily Record 10-12-1949
Miami Daily Record 10-2-1949
Miami Daily Record 9-22-1949

Medford, Oklahoma

Author's interview with Willis Newton
Author's interview with Joe Edward Newton
Author's interview with R.C. Tally
Uvalde County archives – copy of a letter from Edna M Mott to Texas
Ranger Joaquin Jackson dated April 21, 1968 from a Wasco California.
Ada Evening News, 11-28-1932
Ada Evening News, 12-1-1932
Biloxi Daily Herald, 5-13-1934
Clovis NM Evening News Journal, 5-23-1934
El Paso Herald Post, 5-23-1934
Emporia Gazette 4-14-1932
Hutchinson News 4-14-1932
Iola Daily Register 4-14-1932
Jefferson City post Tribune, 4-14-1932
Joplin Globe 5-23-1934
Laredo Times, 12-1-1932
Mason City Globe Gazette, 5-24-1934
Miami Daily News Record, 11-18-1932
Miami Daily News Record, 11-18-1932
Miami Daily News Record, 4-19-1932

Willis Newton

Miami Daily News Record, 5-25-1934
Morning Avalanche, 11-30-1932
Morning Avalanche, 5-30-1934
Salt Lake Tribune 5-5-1934
San Antonio Express, 5-15-1934
Sandusky Star Journal, 5-23-1934
Santa Fe New Mexican, 6-4-1934

Tulsa Shooting

Author's interview with Willis Newton
Author's interview with R.C. Tally
Author's interview with Joe Edward Newton
Ada Weekly News 10-2-1949, 10-6-1949, 9-22-1949
Billings Gazette 6-14-1949
Miami Daily Record 9-22-1949, 10-2-1949, 10-12-1949

Frank Brent & the Big Diamond

Author's interview with Willis Newton
Author's interview with R.C. Tally
Author's interview with Joe Edward Newton
Author's interview with Kenneth Kelley
Ada Evening News 8-1-1962, 8-7-1962
Ada Evening News 4-23-1963, 10-20-1963
Corpus Christi Times 4-23-1963, 10-21-1963
El Paso Herald Post 10-5-1962
Galveston Daily News 11-7-1963
Lawton Constitution 3-7-1963, 4-24-1963
 San Antonio Express 3-26-1963, 3-28-1963, 10-20-1963

Rowena Bank Job

Author's interview with Willis Newton
Author's interview with R.C. Tally
Author's interview with Joe Edward Newton
Author's interview with Kenneth Kelley
Abilene Reporter News 3-5 1968 - page 1 & 8A
Abilene Reporter News 3-6 1968 page 1 & 3A
Abilene Reporter News 8-30 1968
Abilene Reporter News 9-12 1968
Abilene Reporter News 9-14 1968
Amarillo Globe times 11-21-1968

Brownwood Bulletin 3-1 1968
Brownwood Herald 3-5 1968
Corpus Christi Times 3-1-1968
Daily Capital News 3-3-1968
Jefferson City Post Tribune 3-5-1968
Newton Gang Rides Again - Life Mag 1968
Port Arthur News 3-5-1968 page 1 & 2
Victoria Advocate 3-6-1968

Death of the Newton Gang

Author's interview with Willis Newton
Author's interview with R.C. Tally
Author's interview with Joe Edward Newton
Author's interview with Kenneth Kelley

Bibliography

In writing a book of this type, it was important to validate the large volume of information supplied by Willis Newton to me and other interviewers. In addition to interviewing others who had direct information on Willis Newton, this required reading a large volume of different references and compiling an easily read narrative without turning the work into a dry lifeless dissertation. Source materials are listed below:

CITED INTERVIEWS:

Dates of interviews appear in parentheses. All interviews were conducted in person by the author, except where noted.

Hayden Griffin Haby and wife, Doris (July 9, 2010).
Mr. Haby went to school with Joe Edward Newton, the son of Joe Newton. In addition, his family's ranch hired Jess Newton to work cattle and allowed Mr. Haby to taste Jess's campfire cuisine and hear his tales about his life as an outlaw.
Harrison Hamer, 3rd (February 9, 12 2012)
He is the great grandson of the Texas Ranger, Harrison Hamer – who contrary to newspaper reports of the day, was the actual lawman to snap handcuffs on Jess Newton in 1924.

Harrison, Bud, Bobbie Hamer (interviewed by Robert Nieman) (2006).
Oral History Interview with Texas Ranger Descendants. Texas Ranger Hall of Fame and Museum.
Kenneth Kelley (February 24, 2012)
Former Uvalde County sheriff Kenneth Kelley knew all the Newton brothers very well. Kelley moved to Uvalde after World War II and he was working at a service station in Uvalde when he first met Willis Newton in 1948. Willis drove in and asked Kelley to check the air in the tires of his Cadillac. When Kelley opened the trunk to put air in the spare tire, Kelley was "flabbergasted with what he found in the trunk - a big tub of silver dollars."
Joe Edward Newton (February 24 & 27, 2012)
Mr. Newton was the only child of Joe Newton and known in the family as "Little Joe." He provided information on Willis' operations in Tulsa and the Medford Oklahoma bank robbery. He also corroborated the episode where his father taken in by a con-artist.
J. Willis Newton (March 1979)
Reluctant at first, Willis Newton recited a rapid fire, well-rehearsed version of his life, providing detailed accounts of his family and his criminal career. He

wound up letting me copy some of his family pictures.
R.C. Talley (September 10, 2012)
Mr. Talley is the only remaining member of the Newton Gang that is still alive. He was more than willing to tell the "complete" story of the 1968 Rowena bank robbery.

Newspaper Articles:

Ada Evening News
4-23-1963
8-1-1962
8-7-1962
10-20-1963
11-28-1932
Amarillo Globe
"Train Bandit Chief Tried to Kill to Confederates?" November 20, 1924.
11-21-1968
Abilene Reporter News
3-1-1968
3-5-1968 page 1 & 8
3-6-1968 page 1 & 3
8-30-1968
9-12-1968
9-14 1968
Appleton Post-Crescent, Appleton, Wisconsin
"Bandits Shoot Messengers in Street Holdup." July 24, 1923.
Alton Evening Telegraph
6-18-1924
6-21-1924
8-27-1924
11-25-1924
11-18-1924
Associated Press Reports
"Has $100,000 Insurance." March 10, 1922.
"Officers Searched Hills for $100,000 Loot And Robbers." March 10, 1922.
"Bandits Burn Auto In Eluding Pursuit by Toronto Police." July 25, 1923.
"Officers Searched Hills for $100,000 Loot And Robbers." March 10, 1922.
"Payroll Is Taken" March 10, 1921
Bakersfield Morning Echo
6-13-1924 page 1 & 2
Billings Gazette
6-14-1924 page 1 & 2

Bluefield Daily Telegraph
1-3-1925
Brownwood Bulletin
"Fourth Brother Is Taken to Chicago for Mail Robbery." Sept 4, 1924.
"Man in Chicago Train Robbery Once Lived near Town of Eastland." July 1, 1924.
"Yeggs Fail in Effort to Rob Winters Bank; Telephone Cables Cut." March 5, 1919.
3-1 1968
Buffalo Sunday Express
"TAX ASSESSOR IS HELD FOR MAIL ROBBERY. Suspected of being implicated in hiding of $100,000 loot taken from train." April 12, 1925
Bradford Era
4-13-1925
Brownville Herald
"Robbery Still A Mystery." Oct. 4, 1921.
 3-5 1968
Carbondale Free Press
6-13-1924
6-14-1924
6-16-1924
6-17-1924
8-27-1924
11-25-1924
Corpus Christi Times
4-23-1963, 10-21-1963, 3-1-1968,
Chicago Daily Tribune
"$1 Million Train Robbery Near City." June 13, 1924.
"Recover Part of Mail Loot. Six Arrested: One Is Dying; Woman Talks. Two Identified By Clerk Victims." June 15, 1924.
"Seek Dead Bandit as Clew." June 14, 1924.
LeRoux, Charles. "The Bank Robber" Joe Newton Remembers The Old Days."
Chicago Times Herald
"Million Taken from Mail Car by Robber Gang - 40 Patches of Registered Mail Scooped up from Milwaukee Flyer." June 12, 1924.
Connersville News – Examiner
"No Trace Found of Bank Bandits." November 7, 1923.
Dallas Morning News
Biffle, Kent "Damn Fool Robber Recalls Years On The Lam.". June 03, 1985.
Daily Globe
12-31-1925

Daily Herald
7-4-1924 page 1 & 10
9-5-1924
Davenport Democrat and Leader
6-13-1924
Daily Capital News
3-3-1968
Denton Record Chronicle
"Murderous Holdup of Bank Messengers Is Staged in Toronto." July 24, 1923.
"$500,000 Robbery At Denison." August 25, 1921.
"Daring Holdup of Passenger Train Nets Big Fortune." June 13, 1924.
"Two Masked Robbers Hold Up Katy limited, Rifle Postal Cars and Make Their Escape." Aug. 25, 1921.
Decatur Daily Review
6-13-1924
6-19-1924
6-21-1924
6-22-1924
8-27-1924
8-29-1924
11-5-1924
11-12-1924
11-13-1924
11-14-1924
11-18-1924
11-21-1924
11-25-1924
12-6-1924
"Bandits Hold Up Fast Dixie Flyer; Secure Only $400." November 8, 1921.
Dallas Times Herald
MacCormack, John. "What do I care if I am a train robber or not?" Last Bandit Brother A Reluctant Legend." October 20, 1986.
Evening Independent, St. Petersburg, Florida
"Mail Robby Loot Sought By Officers." Jan 1, 1925.
June 6, 1980 (page 5)
Edwardsville Intelligencer
6-19-1924
7-8-1924
8-27-1924 page 1 &2
8-27-1924
8-28-1924

El Paso Herald Post
10-5-1962
Floresville Chronicle
Hamer, Harrison H. "Texas Ranger Harrison Lester Hamer." March 31, 2005.
Elyria Chronicle Telegram
6-14-1924
Fayette County Leader
11-27-1924
Jefferson City Post Tribune
4-14-1932
3-5-1968
Hill Country Herald
Carnegie, Elaine Padgett. "IT WAS JUST BUSINESS...THE NEWTON BROTHERS OF UVALDE TEXAS." December 18, 2010.
Houston Post
Lewis, Glenn. "The Notorious Newtons." February 3, 1980.
Houston Chronicle
Stowers, Carlton. "Audacious Odyssey / The Newton brothers' 1920s crime spree stretched from Texas to Toronto, but they never killed a soul.", Nov. 23, 1997.
Harrison Times
4-24-1925
Hondo Anvil Herald
"Yeggs Rob Hondo Banks." Jan. 12, 1921.
Houston Daily News
"Accused Held for Grand Jury. Examining Trial for Alleged Train Robbery Last Three Days." February 3, 1915.
Galveston Daily News
"Robber Heel May Lead to Arrest." January 11, 1921.
"Boerne Bank Is Robbed of Bonds." February 9, 1921.
"Arrested Held For Grand Jury" Feb. 2, 1915
"Bandits Hold Up Passenger Train; Mail Car Looted." Sept. 7, 1921.
"Bandits Hold Up Train Near Denison Early This Moring." Aug. 25, 1921.
"Boerne Bank Is Robbed of Bonds - Night Watchman Is Forced to Witness Operations of Bandits." February 9, 1921
"District Court Meets." Jan 4, 1916.
"Has Planned to Get at Loot First. Will Reveal Cash of $100,000 Obtained in Rondout Robbery For 20 Years of Liberty." December 13, 1924.
"Katie Train Robbed Crewmembers Tied." October 27, 1921.
"Marble Falls Bank Robbed With Daring." Oct. 27, 1915.
"No Clew to Houston Bank Bandits Has Been Found." Jan. 22, 1921
"Will Reveal Cache of $100,000 Obtained in Rondout Robbery for 20 Years

of Liberty." Dec. 13, 1924.
11-7-1963
12-13-1924
3-17-1919
3-6-1919
3-7-1919
3-6-1919
12-13-1924
3-7-1919
3-17-1919
Indianapolis Star
6-14-1924 page 1 & 9
6-18-1924
6-19-1924 page 1 & 2
6-19-1924
Iola Daily Register
11-15-1924
11-29-1924
Iowa City Press Citizen
12-02-1924
Jefferson City Post Tribune
3-5-1968
Joplin Globe
6-11-1925
6-13-1924 page 1 &2
6-13-1924
6-14-1924
11-20-1924
12-12-1924
Journal and Republican, Lowville, N.Y.
"FAMOUS SLEUTH JAILED FOR HUGE POSTAL ROBBERY." Sept. 11, 1924.
Kokomo Tribune
6-13-1924 page 1 & 16
12-17-1924
Laredo Times
1-8-1915
Laurel Daily Leader
6-16-1924
Lawton Constitution
3-7-1963
4-24-1963

Lethbridge Daily Herald
"Bandits Get Away." July 25, 1923.
Linton Daily Citizen
"Two Spencer Banks Robbed Today." November 6, 1923.
Livingston Daily Sun
"Large Band of Robbers Blow Two Indiana Banks." November 7, 1923.
"Large Band of Robbers Blow Two Indiana Banks - 14 to 20 Men in Party,
Which Traveled In Four Automobiles." November 7, 1923.
Logansport Pharos Tribune
12-15-1925
Louise Freed Alton Evening Telegraph
9-8-1924
Lowell Sun
8-27-1924
Manitoba Free Press
"Car Used by Toronto Bank Bandits Found." July 30, 1923.
"Thinks He Ran Across Toronto Bank Bandits." July 27, 1923.
"Toronto Bank Robbery Loss Put at $125,000." July 25, 1923
Mexia Evening News
"Auto Bandits Rob Postal Sub-Station in Dallas; Get $30,000." Jan. 15, 1921.
Medford Patriot Star
"Two Bandits Rob First National Bank Here" April 14, 1932.
Miami Daily News
"$100,000 Rondout Mail Loot Bonds' Recovered. Arkansas Mail Box Yields
$79,000 Spoils After Mystery Phone Call." Jan. 3, 1925.
4-14-1932 page 1 & 5
4-19-1932
11-18-1932
11-28-1932
Moberly Weekly Monitor
"Bandits Escape With $130,000." July 26, 1923.
"Bandits Kill Bank Messenger." July 26, 1923
Morning Avalanche – Lubbock
"Fahy To Take Stand Today." Nov. 22, 1924.
"Officers Believe Bank Robbery Carried out by Professionals" Jan. 6, 1924
Murphysboro Daily Independent
6-14-1924
8-29-1924
National Star
"Texas Terrors Pull off America's Biggest Train Robbery." July 1974.
Nevada State Journal
11-18-1924

New Braunfels Herald
"Zeitung Version of 1922 Bank Robbery Here Told." July 19, 1973
Hass, Oscar. "Role of Texas Rangers in City's History Recalled." July 12, 1973.
Haas, Oscar. "Zeitung Version of 1922 Bank Robbery Here Told." New Braunfels Herald July 19, 1973.
New Castle News
8-27-1924 page 1 & 5, 2-4-1925
New York Times
BANDITS GET $130,000 IN A RAID ON TORONTO; SHOOT 4 ON STREETS; Six Highwaymen in Car Rout Fourteen Bank Messengers -- Two May Die. July 25, 1923
"OFFER $10,000 REWARD FOR TORONTO BANDITS; Canadian Officials Believe Gang Reached Buffalo -- Wounded Messenger Recovering." July 24, 1923.
"Bank Robbers Find Uvalde Life A Steal." September 21, 1982.
"When Heist Was Nice. Bank robber recalls the good old days when bad guys still wore white hats." July 10, 1980.
Ogden Standard Examiner
11-10-1924
Port Arthur News
"Dying Man May Convict Seven." Nov. 9, 1924
"Mail Bandits Go To Pen." Dec. 12, 1924.
3-5-1968 page 1 &2
Riverdale Pointer
11-28-1924, 1-16-1925
San Angelo Standard Times
"Habeas Corpus Hearing Slated in Bank Break-in." March 5, 1968.
"Rowena Bank Jobs Suspects Are Released." March 7, 1968.
Batten, Jim. "Rondout Heist Netted $3 Million." find citation.
Reed, Joe. "Newton Gang's Exploits Told by Runnels Prisoner." May 5, 1968.
Reed, Joe. "Rowena Shootout Ends With Arrest." March 1, 1968.
San Antonio Light
"30 Day Extradition Stay Won by Newton." August 2, 1924.
"Mail Robbers Get $500,000 in Loot in Texas Hold-Up." Aug. 25, 1921.
"Newton is Lodged in Chicago Prison With His Brothers." Sept. 4, 1924.
"Newton's Escorts Report Favorably." Sept. 8, 1924.
"Safety Deposit Box Yields $7000 Mail Loot." Sept. 26, 1924.
"San Marcos Court Goes Into Session." Sept. 26, 1924.
"Search Started for Buried Loot - Officers Believe $400,000 Taken by Newton Gang Hidden Near Here" October 20, 1925.
1-1-1915

San Antonio Express News
Lindee, Susan. "Newton Has No Regrets About His Outlawed Days". June 20, 1980
"San Marcos Robbery Laid to Newton Gang." August 17, 1924.
"Pullman Porter Gets Tip." Jan. 1, 1915.
"8 U.S. Officials Face Arrest." June 27, 1924.
"Doc Newton Draws Two-Year Sentence." November 1968.
"Finger Prints May Solve San Marcos Bank Robbery in Which $20,000 Stolen." Jan. 6, 1924.
"Last Train Robber Joe Newton, Dies at 88." February 12, 1989
"Loot Search Starts on Castroville Road." Oct. 21, 1925.
"Men Seen There At The Time of Robbery." Aug. 17, 1924.
"New Braunfels Robbery Recalls Recent Attempt to Rob First National." March 10, 1922.
"Safes In Karnes City and Bandera Blown." Dec. 6, 1921.
"Search For Buried Loot." San Antonio Express Oct. 20, 1925.
"Sleuths Strike Snag in Search for Bandits - Hope of Connecting Two Men at Dallas with Robbery Fails." Feb. 14, 1921.
"State and Federal Courts Clash Over Jurisdiction." June 27, 1924.
"Texas Killer Sought As Mail Bandit; Four Alleged Robbers Held." June 19, 1924.
"Two Bandits Awaken and Rob Passengers on Southern Pacific - Obtain $7840 And Many Valuables; Overlook $16,000." Jan. 1, 1915.
Stinson, Roddy. "Willis and Joe: Outlaws From the Past." March 16, 1976.
West, Tommy – Trails West. "Last of the Robbers' Lives Quiet, Easy Life." November 11, 1984
3-26-1963
3-28-1963
10-20-1963
7-30-1924
8-27-1924 page 1 & 3
1-1-1925
1-3-1925
2-26-1925
4-17-1925
3-17-1919
San Antonio Evening News
"Sleuths Strike Snag in Search for Bandits." February 14, 1921
Massey, J.F., "The Daring Newton Gang." November 14, 1924.
Southwest Texas New Service, San Marcos
"Newton Gang Hit Sam Marcos."
Steubenville Herald
8-27-1924

8-28-1924
Thomasville Times Enterprises
2-14-1925
Titusville Herald
1-3-1925
Toledo Blade
LeRoux, Charles. "Joe Newton, Last of the Outlaws." April 5, 1981.
Traverse City Record Eagle
11-25-1924
Tucson Daily Citizen
10-1-1925
Tulsa World
Curtis, Gene. "Robbery Just Another Business for Tulsan." Nov. 27, 2006.
Victoria Advocate
3-6-1968
Washington Times
"Most Daring Bandit in American History." July 20, 1902
Washington Post
8-28-1924
Wichita Daily Times
1-1-1915
Wisconsin Rapids Daily Tribune
11-18-1924
11-29-1924
3-25-1925
Waterloo Evening Courier
8-27-1924 page 1 & 2
Uvalde Leader News
"FOUR NEWTONS PEAD GUILTY - Were Accused of Being in $2 Million Mail Robbery in Illinois." November 14, 1924.
"Newtons Returned to Scene of Crime."– February 8, 1977
"Uvalde Man Convicted in Oklahoma." November 10, 1963.
Jess Newton – death notice. March 6, 1960
Rambie, Margaret. "Folklife Festival to Feature Five Uvalde Frontiersmen." Uvalde Leader News, July 24, 1980.
Rambie, Margaret. "Joe Newton's Death Marks End of Era" Uvalde Leader News, February 5, 1989
Wylie "Doc" Newton Death notice. Sept. 29, 1974.
Zavala County Sentinel
Notice of Newton brothers release from jail. September 9, 1909.

Willis Newton

Magazine Articles

Dingus, Anne. "The Newton Boys." *Texas Monthly Magazine*. May (1998).

Applebome, Peter. "The Great Train Robber." *Texas Monthly Magazine*. September (1982).

Snell, David. "The Newton Gang Rides Again" *Life Magazine* April 19, 1968.

Maguire, Jack. "The Texas Terrors - Four Others from Uvalde Become the Most Successful Train Robbers Ever." Southwest Airlines Magazine July 1984.
Hynd, Alan and Joseph Millard. "Twisted Track Down of the Train Robbers." True – The Man's Magazine - March, 1960

Hagy, Marjorie. "A Crime For The Ages." Online magazine marjorie@hillcountryexplore.com

Macht, Norman L. "Newton Gang Played It Safe - Robbery was big-time business for these Texas outlaws." Texas Co-op Power Online Magazine, October Issue 2008
Massey, J.F. "The Daring Newton Gang." Vol. 22, #6, March 1945.
"Tells of the Rondout Robbery." Frontier Times Magazine, Vol. 9, # 4, January 1932.

BOOKS

Boerne Citizens State Bank History. Boerne Public Library files.
Clarahan, Donald. The Great Rondout Train Robbery. Norfolk-Hall, Bloomington, Ill. 1980
Rios, J. A. Hondo Bank Robbery. History of Medina County.
Stanush, Claude and David Middleton. The Portrait of an Outlaw Gang. State House Press, 1994.
Walker, Donald R. Penology for Profit: A History of the Texas Prison System, 1867–1912 (College Station: Texas A&M University Press, 1988).

Personal Accounts

Goff, Myra Lee Adams. "A Bank robbery in Downtown New Braunfels."

ONLINE NEWSPAPERS

NYDailyNews.com "The Last American Desperado" Sunday, June 17, 2007.

Sun-Times News Group newsunonline.com
Finley, Larry. "Wounded Rondout Schoolgirl Carried Train Robbery Bullet for Rest of Her Life - Girl was shot on way to school as historic heist of 1924 played out." Friday, July 13, 2007.

TELEVISION PROGRAMS

The Newton Boys: Portrait of an Outlaw Gang Documentary film. Jack Landman, 1976.
Tonight Show with Johnny Carson. Joe Newton as guest. October 1980.
Real Newton Boys. Documentary film, Kroopnick, Stephen; Schreiberg, Stu; Raven, Abbe; Werbe, Susan. 1975.

Photo Sources

City of Toronto Archives
Denver Public Library (Western History Collection)
Historic New Orleans Collection
J. Willis Newton
Jane Brummett
Kansas State Historical Society, Topeka.
Kenneth Kelley
Library of Congress
Nevada Historical Society
Old Time Texas Collection
R.C. Talley
San Antonio Public Library, Texas/Genealogy
State of Arizona, Library Archives and Public Records Division
Texas State Library and Archives
University of Illinois Archives
UTSA, Institute of Texan Cultures
U.S. National Archives and Records Administration
Western History Collections, University of Oklahoma

Index

Holliday, Herbert, 39, 43, 99, 100, 130, 133, 151, 160, 168, 172, 173, 174, 221
Hondo, Texas, 46

J

Jackson, Norman, 97, 98
James, Frank & Jesse, 61
Johns, Anthony N., 117
Johnson, Red, 100

K

Kelley, Sheriff Kenneth, 199, 229, 234
Knowlton, J.H., 124

L

Lard, Alan, 85
Leavenworth Prison, 172, 179
Lisso, Butch, 208

M

Madero, Benjamin, 106
Mammy, 215
Mammy", 197
Martinez, Jose, 103
McAlester Prison, 190
McComb, Walter, 149
McKinney, J.C., 173
Medford, Oklahoma, 187
Melita, Manitoba, 57
Menger Hotel, 42
Moon, Arthur, 124, 125
Moosomin, Saskatchewan, 57
Moss, E., 116
Murphy, "Big Tim", 157
Murray, James, 129, 146, 153, 165, 167, 170, 221
Music Box Club, 196
Mustang Island, Texas, 196

N

New Braunfels, Texas, 64
Newton Gangs' Getaway, 99

Newton, "Little Joe", 191, 195, 196, 223, 234
Newton, Henry, 16
Newton, Ivy, 16
Newton, Janetta, 19, 32
Newton, Jim, 16
Newton, Joseph Edward, 187
Newton, Louise, 147, 151, 185, 193
Newton, Tull, 35
Norton, Dora, 18

O

Oaks Country Club, 194
O'Banion, Dean, 149, 221
Oglesby, Neal, 201
Omaha, Nebraska, 44

P

Paxton, Illinois, 119
Pearsall, Texas, 56
Phillips, Lewis, 142
Poe, Tom, 173

R

Rankins, Charlie, 12
Robles kidnapping, 191
Rondout historical marker, 177
Rondout Mail Train Robbery, 129
Rowena Bank Job, 205
Rowena, Texas, 205
Ruppert, George, 207
Rusk Prison, 30, 235

S

San Marcos, Texas, 94
Schoemaker, Captain William, 146, 152, 175
Shangri-La Club, 196
Sheets, John, 61
Short, Benedict, 166
Simmons, Rush D., 152
Spencer, Indiana, 88
St. Joseph, Missouri, 126
Stable Club, 196

ABOUT THE AUTHOR

G.R. Williamson lives in the Texas Hill Country near Kerrville with his wife, Jean, and his ever faithful Chihuahua, "Shooter". He is a historical researcher, a historian and a born storyteller. As a child, he grew up hearing his granddad and his bluegrass-playing buddies spin yarns under shade trees between sets. He would sit and wonder at their ability to peel pecans with their knives and then eat the pecans, all the while chewing tobacco. It was a true wonder to behold.

Then later he was fortunate enough to encounter a number of storytelling sages to engender a real passion for the art form.

Over the years he has written several books and many articles on Texas historical figures and events in Texas history. In addition, he has penned several western motion picture screenplays. His current book on Willis Newton stems from an interview he had with the outlaw shortly before he died at age 90—and was still an unrepentant outlaw.

For more information, visit his website OldTimeTexas.com.

www.ingramcontent.com/pod-product-compliance
Lightning Source LLC
Chambersburg PA
CBHW060300100426
42742CB00011B/1820